Keys to Learning

Skills and Strategies for Newcomers

Workbook

Anna Uhl Chamot

Catharine W. Keatley

Kristina Anstrom

with

Charles Green

Longman

Keys to Learning

Skills and Strategies for Newcomers

Workbook

Pearson Education, 10 Bank Street, White Plains, NY 10606

Vice president, primary and secondary editorial: Ed Lamprich
Publisher: Sherri Pemberton
Senior development editor: Barbara Barysh
Vice president, director of production and design: Rhea Banker
Senior production editor: Jane Townsend
Vice president, U.S. marketing: Kate McLoughlin
Senior manufacturing buyer: Edith Pullman
Photo research: Kirchoff/Wohlberg, Inc.
Cover design: Rhea Banker, Tara Mayer Raucci
Text design and composition: Kirchoff/Wohlberg, Inc.
Text font: ITC Franklin Gothic
Illustration and photo credits: See page 204.

ISBN: 0-13-189223-1

Printed in the United States of America
5 6 7 8 9 10–VHG–08 07

ESL

Contents

Introduction

Getting Started

INTRODUCTIONS

A. Write your first name and your last name.

Example: *Anita Sanchez*

_____	_____
first name	**last (family) name**

B. Complete the dialogue. Use words from the box.

nice	name	Hello	What's	meet	Hi

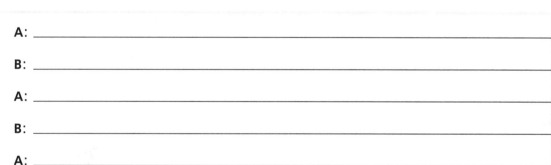

A: (**1**) _____*Hello.*_____ .

B: (**2**) _____ . (**3**) _____ your name?

A: My (**4**) _____ is Thomas Molina.

B: I'm Ms. Evans. Nice to (**5**) _____ you, Thomas.

A: (**6**) _____ to meet you, too.

C. Write the dialogue from Exercise **B**. You are person **A**. Use *Ms.*, *Mrs.*, or *Mr.* with your teacher's name.

A: _____

B: _____

A: _____

B: _____

A: _____

Name _____ Date _____

CLASSROOM OBJECTS

A. Look at the pictures. Write the names of the objects. Use words from the box.

a bookcase	a table	a chair	a desk	a book
a notebook	a pen	a pencil	an eraser	

1. _____a notebook_____

2. _____

3. _____

4. _____

5. _____

6. _____

7. _____

8. _____

9. _____

B. Write the dialogues. Use words from Exercise A.

1.

A: _____What's this?_____

B: _____It's a pencil._____

2.

A: _____

B: _____

3.

A: _____

B: _____

CLASSROOM COMMANDS

A. Look at the pictures. Write the commands for the actions you see. Use commands from the box.

Raise your hand.	Write your name.	Get your pen.
Stand up.	Close your book.	Open your notebook.

1. _____Get your pen._____ **2.** _____ **3.** _____

4. _____ **5.** _____ **6.** _____

B. Follow the commands.

Get your pencil.

1.

Get your notebook.

2.

Open your notebook.

3.

Write your first
and last name.

4.

Write your teacher's name.
Use *Ms.*, *Mrs.*, or *Mr.*

5.

Close your notebook.

6.

Name _____ Date _____

DAYS OF THE WEEK

A. Complete the chart. Write the days in order.

Weekdays	Weekend Days
1. _____Monday_____ Thursday	6. _____ Saturday
2. _____ Monday	7. _____ Sunday
3. _____ Wednesday	
4. _____ Friday	
5. _____ Tuesday	

B. Fill in the blanks. Write the day of the week. Write true sentences.

1. Today is _____.

2. Tomorrow is _____.

C. Write the days of the week in order.

THE ALPHABET

A. Write the alphabet. Fill in the blanks. Use capital and small letters.

1. A *a*	**7.** G ____	**13.** M ____	**19.** S ____	**25.** Y ____
2. *B* b	**8.** ____ h	**14.** ____ n	**20.** ____ t	**26.** ____ z
3. C ____	**9.** I ____	**15.** O ____	**21.** U ____	
4. ____ d	**10.** ____ j	**16.** ____ p	**22.** ____ v	
5. E ____	**11.** K ____	**17.** Q ____	**23.** W ____	
6. ____ f	**12.** ____ l	**18.** ____ r	**24.** ____ x	

B. Complete the alphabet. Use small letters.

			d					
	k							*r*
				x				

C. Write the names of four friends or people in your family. Ask "How do you spell your name?"

1. _____ *Mei Song* _____

2. _____

3. _____

4. _____

5. _____

Introduction Getting Started

5

Name _____ Date _____

NUMBERS 1-20

A. Complete the puzzle. Write the number words. Use words from the box.

| eight | three | one | six | four | nine | seven | ten | two | five |

B. Write the number words. Use words from the box.

| fifteen | nineteen | twelve | twenty | seventeen |
| eighteen | thirteen | sixteen | eleven | fourteen |

11 ___eleven___   15 _____   18 _____

12 _____   16 _____   19 _____

13 _____   17 _____   20 _____

14 _____

C. Write the answers. Then rewrite the math problems. Use number words.

1. 18−7 = _11_   _____eighteen − seven = eleven_____

2. 6+13 = ___   _____

3. 17−5 = ___   _____

Introduction Getting Started

NUMBERS 20–100

A. Write the number words. Use words from the box.

forty	ninety	thirty	seventy	eighty
one hundred	sixty	fifty	twenty	

20 _____	**50** _____	**80** _____
30 _____	**60** _sixty_	**90** _ninety_
40 _forty_	**70** _____	**100** _____

B. Write the prices of the items.

1. _sixty-nine dollars_   2. _____   3. _____

4. _____   5. _____   6. _____

C. Write the answers. Then rewrite the math problems. Use number words.

1. 22 + 62 = _84_   _twenty-two + sixty-two = eighty-four_

2. 94 − 41 = ___   _____

3. 39 + 57 = ___   _____

4. 76 − 48 = ___   _____

5. 26 + 74 = ___   _____

Name _____ Date _____

A. Look at the clocks. Write the time. Use words from the box.

| oh five   fifteen   forty-five   o'clock   thirty |

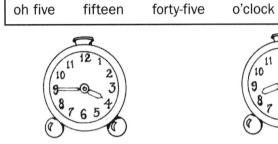

1. three _*forty-five*_   **2.** eight _____   **3.** two _____

4. nine _____   **5.** five _____

B. Look at the pictures. Complete the dialogues.

1. A: What time is it?

   B: _*It's six forty-five.*_

2. A: What time is it?

   B: _____

3. A: What time is it?

   B: _____

4. A: What time is it?

   B: _____

C. Look at the pictures in exercise B again. Write the time you do the activities.

1. _7:00_   **2.** _____   **3.** _____   **4.** _____

MONTHS OF THE YEAR

A. Circle the months of the year.

J	A	N	U	A	R	Y	A	J	F	O	N	Q	A	L
S	E	P	T	E	M	B	E	R	E	C	O	A	P	W
M	A	R	C	H	J	Y	W	I	B	T	V	U	R	D
S	U	M	X	U	A	L	X	O	R	O	E	G	I	J
S	R	A	L	M	G	T	K	J	U	B	M	U	L	U
Y	H	Y	M	C	U	N	R	U	A	E	B	S	A	N
D	E	C	E	M	B	E	R	L	R	R	E	T	G	E
S	D	C	P	Y	U	L	T	Y	Y	M	R	F	A	X

B. Write the months of the year from Exercise A on the calendar.

_____   _____   _March_____   _____

_____   _____   _____   _August_____

_September____   _____   _____   _____

DATES (ORDINAL NUMBERS 1ˢᵗ – 31ˢᵗ)

A. Fill in the sentences with the ordinal number. Then write the number word in the puzzle.

ACROSS

3. November is the _11th_ month of the year.

4. May is the ____ month of the year.

7. February is the ____ month of the year.

8. June is the ____ month of the year.

9. October is the ____ month of the year.

10. December is the ____ month of the year.

DOWN

1. April is the ____ month of the year.

2. March is the ____ month of the year.

3. August is the ____ month of the year.

4. January is the ____ month of the year.

5. July is the ____ month of the year.

6. September is the ____ month of the year.

B. Complete the calendar. Write the missing ordinal numbers in the boxes.

Sunday	Monday	Tuesday	Wednesday	Thursday	Friday	Saturday
		1ˢᵗ				
		first	second	third	fourth	fifth
6ᵗʰ				10ᵗʰ		
sixth	seventh	eighth	ninth	tenth	eleventh	twelfth
	14ᵗʰ					
thirteenth	fourteenth	fifteenth	sixteenth	seventeenth	eighteenth	nineteenth
			23ʳᵈ			
twentieth	twenty-first	twenty-second	twenty-third	twenty-fourth	twenty-fifth	twenty-sixth
	28ᵗʰ		30ᵗʰ			
twenty-seventh	twenty-eighth	twenty-ninth	thirtieth	thirty-first		

Chapter 1

What's your name?

LISTENING AND READING

Read "Good Morning" on Student Book
pages 18–19. Then complete each sentence.
Circle the letter of the correct answer.

1. Mr. Gomez speaks ___.

   a. English   **b.** English and Spanish

2. Carlos and ___ are brother and sister.

   a. Carmen   **b.** Maria

3. They are from ___.

   a. Mexico   **b.** the United States

4. ___ is very nervous.

   a. Maria   **b.** Carmen

VOCABULARY

A. Complete each sentence. Use a word from the box.

brother   okay   teacher   students

1. Mr. Gomez is the _____*teacher*_____.

2. Bic, Carmen, Carlos, and Maria are _____.

3. Carmen and Carlos are sister and _____.

4. Mr. Gomez asks Maria, "Are you _____?"

B. Complete each sentence. Write about yourself.

My name is (**1**) _____.

I'm from (**2**) _____. I speak (**3**) _____

and (**4**) _____.

Name _____   Date _____

Grammar 1

Pronouns

A. Look at the pictures. Write the correct pronoun. Use a word from the box.

| I | he | she | it | we | they |

1. _____we_____

2. _____

3. _____

4. _____

5. _____

6. _____

B. Fill in the blanks with the correct pronouns.

1. the pencil ⟶ _____it_____   4. Carlos and Carmen ⟶ _____

2. Carlos ⟶ _____   5. Maria and I ⟶ _____

3. Maria ⟶ _____   6. Maria and you ⟶ _____

C. Write the sentences again. Use pronouns.

1. <u>Mr. Gomez</u> is the English teacher. ⟶ *He is the English teacher.*

2. <u>Bic and Carlos</u> are students. ⟶ _____

3. <u>Bic, Carlos, and I</u> are students. ⟶ _____

4. <u>The pen</u> is new. ⟶ _____

5. <u>You and Carlos</u> are from Mexico. ⟶ _____

6. <u>Carlos and Carmen</u> are brother and sister. ⟶ _____

Grammar 2

Present Tense of *be*: Statements

A. Fill in the blanks with the correct form of *be*.

1. You _____*are*_____ from Mexico.

2. I _____ a student.

3. She _____ Carmen.

4. He _____ Carlos.

5. They _____ teachers.

6. We _____ brother and sister.

7. It _____ a backpack.

8. Mr. Gomez _____ a teacher.

9. Maria _____ pretty.

10. Carlos and Carmen _____ students.

11. I _____ very nervous.

12. You and Maria _____ friends.

B. Fill in the blanks with the correct pronoun and the correct form of *be*. Use contractions.

1. (They are) _____*They're*_____ students.

2. (He is) _____ the English teacher.

3. (It is) _____ a pencil.

4. (I am) _____ from Peru.

5. (You are) _____ from the United States.

C. Change each statement from the affirmative to the negative. Use contractions.

1. He is nervous. ⟶ _____*He's not nervous.*_____

2. I am twelve. ⟶ _____

3. We are from the United States. ⟶ _____

4. She is my teacher. ⟶ _____

5. They are brother and sister. ⟶ _____

6. You are my brother. ⟶ _____

Word Study

The Alphabet

Complete the charts. Use capital and small letters.

A B *C* ___ E ___ G H ___ J K L ___ ___ O ___ Q R ___ ___ U V ___ X Y ___

a ___ c d ___ f g ___ i ___ k ___ m n ___ p ___ ___ s t ___ v w x ___ z

Consonants and Vowels

A. Write the consonants.

b ___ ___ ___ ___ ___ ___ ___ ___ ___

___ ___ ___ ___ ___ ___ ___ ___ ___ ___

B. Write the vowels.

a ___ ___ ___ ___

C. Fill in the blanks. Use the letters in the box.

a	e	i
k	r	t	y

1. I sp *e* *a* *k* English.

2. His n ___ m ___ is Carlos.

3. His s ___ s ___ ___ r is Carmen.

4. Are you o ___ a ___ ?

5. My te ___ ch ___ ___ is Mr. Gomez.

6. Bic and Carmen are s ___ ud ___ n ___ s.

Alphabetical Order

Write the words in the box in alphabetical order in your notebook.

pretty	students	brother	sister	he
okay	English	teacher	name	nice

1. _____ *brother* _____   2. _____ *English* _____

Grammar 3

Present Tense of *be*: Yes/No Questions

A. Change each statement to a question.

1. You are a student. ⟶ *Are you a student?* _____

2. They are pretty. ⟶ _____

3. He is nervous. ⟶ _____

4. It is a pencil. ⟶ _____

5. She is from El Salvador. ⟶ _____

B. Complete the questions. Write the correct form of *be*. Then complete the short answers.

1. **A:** *Are* you students?
   B: Yes, *we are*.

2. **A:** *Is* he from Mexico?
   B: No, *he's not*.

3. **A:** _____ they teachers?
   B: No, _____.

4. **A:** _____ she pretty?
   B: Yes, _____.

5. **A:** _____ they nervous?
   B: Yes, _____.

6. **A:** _____ he a new student?
   B: Yes, _____.

7. **A:** _____ it okay?
   B: Yes, _____.

8. **A:** _____ you sisters?
   B: No, _____.

9. **A:** _____ he your brother?
   B: No, _____.

10. **A:** _____ it Saturday?
    B: No, _____.

C. Answer the questions about yourself. Use short answers.

1. Are you nervous? _____.

2. Are you a new student? _____.

3. Are you sixteen? _____.

Reading

A. Read "A New School" on Student Book page 25. Then complete each sentence.
Circle the letter of the correct answer.

1. Maria is from ____.

    a. the United States   **(b.)** El Salvador

2. She's a new ____.

    a. teacher   **b.** student

3. Mr. Gomez is her ____.

    a. brother   **b.** teacher

4. Maria is ____.

    a. nervous   **b.** okay

5. Maria says, ____.

    a. "Nice to meet you."   **b.** "My name is . . ."

6. Carlos says Maria is ____.

    a. a new student   **b.** very pretty

B. Complete each sentence. Use a word from the box.

school	pretty	nice	new	speaks	very

1. Maria is a _____ *new* _____ student at Washington School.

2. She's not okay. She's _____ nervous.

3. Carlos says Maria is very _____.

4. Maria's teacher _____ English.

5. Hello, Maria. My name is Mr. Gomez. _____ to meet you.

6. Maria's new _____ is in the United States.

Writing

BEFORE YOU WRITE

A. Read the paragraph.

> Min Lee is my friend. She is a student at Madison School. She is from Korea. She speaks Korean and English.

B. Read the *Before I Write* checklist. Make notes on the lines below.

Before I Write

▶ Study the model.

▶ Think about a friend.

▶ Make notes about my classroom.

1. My friend's name: _____

2. The name of my friend's school: _____

3. The name of my friend's country: _____

4. The languages my friend speaks: _____

Writing

WRITE THIS!

Read the *While I Write* checklist. Look at your notes from Exercise B and write your paragraph.

While I Write

▶ Put a capital letter at the beginning of a sentence.

She is a student at Madison School.

▶ Put a capital letter at the beginning of the name of a person, place, country, or language.

Min Lee   Korea
Madison School   Korean, English

▶ Put a period at the end of each sentence.

Min Lee is my friend.

AFTER YOU WRITE

A. Read the *After I Write* checklist. Make corrections to your paragraph above.

After I Write

▶ Did I put a capital letter at the beginning of each sentence?

▶ Did I put a capital letter at the beginning of the name of each person, place, country, or language?

▶ Did I put a period at the end of each sentence?

B. Make a final copy of your paragraph in your notebook.

Chapter 2

What classes do you have?

LISTENING AND READING

Read "Our Schedules" on Student Book pages 28–29. Then complete the schedules below. Fill in the blanks with the names of the classes.

Carmen's Schedule	Liliana's Schedule	Maria's Schedule
lunch Cafeteria	**(3)** _____ Gym A	music Room 7
(1) _____ Gym A	**lunch** Cafeteria	**lunch** Cafeteria
math Room 23	math Room 23	math Room 23
(2) _____ Room 12	science Room 12	**(5)** _____ Room 12
music Room 7	**(4)** _____ Room 7	P. E. Gym B

VOCABULARY

Complete each sentence. Use a word from the box.

together   schedules   almost   different   same   after

1. I have Mr. Gomez. You have Mr. Gomez. We have the _____ teacher.

2. I have math now. You have science now. We have _____ classes now.

3. We have English now. Mr. Gomez is our teacher. We have English _____.

4. I have lunch, then music. I have music _____ lunch.

5. We have P.E. and math. Then we have science and lunch. Our _____ are the same.

6. Maria and Liliana have math and science together. Then Maria has P.E. and Liliana has music. Their schedules are _____ the same.

Grammar 1

Present Tense of *have*: Affirmative Statements

A. Complete the sentences. Fill in the blanks with the present tense of *have*.

1. He _____*has*_____ P.E. after science.

2. They _____ math together.

3. She _____ science, then music.

4. You _____ English now.

5. We _____ the same music class.

6. I _____ lunch after science.

B. Read the schedules. Write your name at the top of the third schedule. Then complete each sentence. Use the correct form of *have* and the name of the class.

Anna	Pang	_____
math − Room 16	math − Room 16	math − Room 16
science − Room 22	music − Music A	music − Music A
music − Music A	English − Room 3	science − Room 19
lunch − Cafeteria A	lunch − Cafeteria B	lunch − Cafeteria A
English − Room 3	science − Room 23	English − Room 3
P. E. − Gym B	P. E. − Gym B	history − Room 13

1. Anna _____*has*_____ science after _____*math*_____ .

2. Pang _____ science after lunch. Then he has _____

3. I _____ history and _____ after lunch.

4. Anna and I _____ _____ and _____ together.

5. Pang and Anna _____ _____ and _____ together.

6. Pang and I _____ _____ and _____ together every day.

C. In your notebook, write five sentences about your own schedule. Use *then*, *after*, *together*, *schedule*, and *different*.

Example: *My sister and I have the same schedule.*

Grammar 2

Present Tense of *have*: Negative Statements

Change each sentence from affirmative to negative.
Use *don't have* or *doesn't have*.

1. I have lunch now.   ⟶   I _____*don't have*_____ lunch now.

2. She has seven classes.   ⟶   She _____ seven classes.

3. They have history together.   ⟶   They _____ history together.

4. You have science now.   ⟶   You _____ science now.

5. We have the same schedule.   ⟶   We _____ the same schedule.

Present Tense of *have*: Yes/No Questions

A. Fill in the blanks with *do* or *does*.

1. _____*Do*_____ you and Eva have math together?

2. _____ he have six classes?

3. _____ Anibal have science after math?

4. _____ Min have lunch now?

5. _____ they have the same schedule?

B. Look at the schedules on page 20. Write *yes/no* questions with *have*.
Then write short answers.

1. **A:** *Does Anna have music after P.E.?* _____

   B: *No, she doesn't.* _____

2. **A:** *Do Anna and Pang have P.E. together?* _____

   B: *Yes, they do.* _____

3. **A:** _____

   B: _____

4. **A:** _____

   B: _____

Word Study

Short Vowel Sounds: /a/ as in *cat*, /i/ as in *sit*, /o/ as in *hot*

A. Look at the pictures and sound out the words. Fill in the blanks with *a*, *i*, or *o*.

1. m _a_ p

2. h ___ t

3. p ___ g

4. h ___ t

5. h ___ t

6. c ___ p

7. s ___ x

8. c ___ t

B. Sound out the sentences. Circle (◯) words with the short /i/ sound. Underline
(___) words with the short /o/ sound. Box (☐) words with the short /a/ sound.
When you find one of the words, fill in a star.

1. (It's) not (his) ☐hat☐. ★★★★

2. I have six big caps. ☆☆☆☆

3. The cat has a hat. ☆☆☆

4. The map is not big. ☆☆☆☆

5. Carlos had a big hit with his new bat. ☆☆☆☆☆☆

6. Do you have a big map? ☆☆☆

C. Choose three words from Exercise A. In your notebook, write a sentence using each
word.

Example: *My cat's name is Fluffy.*

Grammar 3

Plural Nouns

Write the plural form of each noun. Add –s or –es.

1. name ⟶ *names*
2. box ⟶ _____
3. lunch ⟶ _____
4. day ⟶ _____
5. cat ⟶ _____

6. class ⟶ _____
7. student ⟶ _____
8. school ⟶ _____
9. brush ⟶ _____
10. schedule ⟶ _____

Possessive Adjectives

A. Fill in the blanks with the correct possessive adjective.

1. You're Clara. _____*Your*_____ name is Clara.

2. She's my sister. _____ name is Kendra.

3. We're students. _____ names are Kim and Ruben.

4. They're our teachers. _____ names are Mr. Ramos and Ms. Chun.

B. Fill in the blanks. Use possessive adjectives from the box.

| my | his | their | her | our |

Hi! (**1**) _____*My*_____ name is Esteban.

I'm from Mexico. This is (**2**) _____ mother.

(**3**) _____ name is Anna. This is

(**4**) _____ father. (**5**) _____ name is

Tomas. This is (**6**) _____ brother and this is

(**7**) _____ sister. (**8**) _____ names are

Manuel and Bettina. We have a cat. (**9**) _____

cat's name is Dusty.

Reading

A. Read "The Math Class" on Student Book pages 34–35. Then complete each sentence. Circle the letter of the correct answer.

1. Mrs. Garcia has ____ students.

   a. five   **b.** nine

2. Carlos ____ math class with Carmen.

   a. has   **b.** doesn't have

3. Mrs. Garcia is from ____.

   a. El Salvador   **b.** Puerto Rico

4. Mei speaks ____.

   a. Spanish   **b.** Chinese

5. The students have math class ____.

   a. every day   **b.** on Monday and Friday

B. Complete each sentence. Use a word from the box.

languages	every	also	favorite	classes

1. We have lunch _____ day.

2. I have three _____ after lunch. I have history, art, and science.

3. Mrs. Garcia speaks two _____. She speaks Spanish and English.

4. I have a brother. I _____ have a sister.

5. Carmen's _____ class is math.

Writing

BEFORE YOU WRITE

A. Read the paragraph.

> Pierre Frank is my friend.
> He is from Africa. He speaks
> French and English. We have
> science and P.E together. We
> don't have lunch together. Pierre
> loves P.E. It is his favorite class.

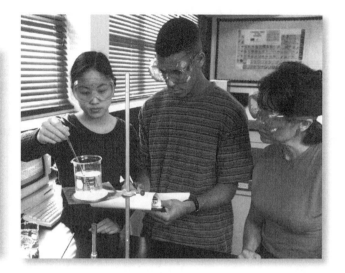

B. Read the *Before I Write* checklist. Make notes on the lines below.

Before I Write

▶ Study the model.

▶ Think about a friend.

▶ Make notes about my classroom.

1. My friend's name: _____

2. My friend's country: _____

3. The language (or languages) my friend speaks: _____

4. The classes we have together: _____

5. My friend's favorite class: _____

Writing

WRITE THIS!

Read the *While I Write* checklist. Look at your notes from Exercise B and write
your paragraph.

While I Write

▶ Put a capital letter at the beginning of a sentence.
   He is from Africa.

▶ Put a capital letter at the beginning of the name of a person, place, country,
   or language.
   Pierre Frank
   Africa
   English, French

▶ Put a period at the end of a sentence.
   We have P.E. and science together.

AFTER YOU WRITE

A. Read the *After I Write* checklist. Make corrections to your paragraph above.

After I Write

▶ Did I put a capital letter at the beginning of each sentence?

▶ Did I put a capital letter at the beginning of the name of each person, place,
   country, or language?

▶ Did I put a period at the end of each sentence?

B. Make a final copy of your paragraph in your notebook.

Chapter 3

This is a calculator.

Read "Maria's Teacher" on Student Book pages 38–39.
Then complete each sentence. Circle the letter of the
correct answer.

1. Some of the English words for math class

   are ___ for Maria.

   a. fine   **b.** hard

2. Carmen has more ___ in her backpack.

   a. things   **b.** calculators

3. The folders are ___.

   a. Carmen's   **b.** not Carmen's

4. Carmen has ten ___ in her wallet.

   a. folders   **b.** dollars

5. Carlos has Carmen's ___.

   a. backpack   **b.** calculator

VOCABULARY

Complete each sentence. Use a word from the box.

borrow	things	calculator	fun	wallet

1. I don't have my eraser. Is it okay if I _____ your eraser?

2. I have five dollars in my _____.

3. I have a lot of _____ in my backpack. I have books, notebooks,

   pens, and pencils.

4. I love music. Music class is _____.

5. The students use a _____ in math class.

Grammar 1

Articles: *a* and *an*

A. Circle the vowels.

a b c d e f g h i j k l m n o p q r s t u v w x (y) z	*sometimes*

B. Write the correct articles on the lines. Write *a* before nouns beginning with consonant sounds. Write *an* before nouns beginning with vowel sounds.

1. _a_ student   5. ___ calculator   9. ___ wallet

2. _an_ idea   6. ___ eraser   10. ___ orange

3. ___ book   7. ___ folder   11. ___ umbrella

4. ___ apple   8. ___ teacher   12. ___ protractor

Demonstrative Pronouns: *this* and *that*

Match each sentence on the left with a picture on the right. Write the letter on the line.

1. _c_ This is an orange.

2. ___ That is an umbrella.

3. ___ This is a backpack.

4. ___ That is an orange.

5. ___ This is an umbrella.

6. ___ That is a backpack.

a

b

c

d

e

f

Grammar 2

Demonstrative Pronouns: *these* and *those*

A. Fill in the blanks with the correct pronoun and verb in parentheses.

1. _____*These are*_____ notebooks. (This is / These are)

2. _____ a protractor. (This is / These are)

3. _____ an apple. (That is / Those are)

4. _____ folders. (This is / These are)

5. _____ math books. (That is / Those are)

6. _____ backpacks. (That is / Those are)

B. Look at the pictures. Write a sentence for each picture. Use words from the box and *this*, *that*, *these*, or *those*.

| boxes | backpack | notebooks | hairbrushes | apple | erasers |

1. _____*That is an apple.*_____

2. _____

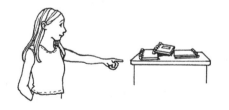

3. _____

4. _____

5. _____

6. _____

Word Study

Short Vowel Sounds: /e/ as in *bed* and /u/ as in *cup*

A. Look at the pictures and sound out the words. Fill in the blanks with *e* or *u*.

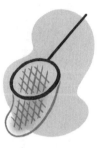

1. b___d

2. b___s

3. p___n

4. n___t

5. s___n

6. t___n

7. d___sk

8. c___p

B. Sound out the words in each list. Check (✔) "yes" if all three words in the list have the same short vowel sound /e/ or same short vowel sound /u/. Check "no" if they do not.

1. pet	**2.** pen	**3.** cup	**4.** run
net	bed	brush	ten
pup	pet	fun	sun
☐ yes ✔ no	☐ yes ☐ no	☐ yes ☐ no	☐ yes ☐ no

C. Choose four words from Exercise A. In your notebook, write a sentence using each word.

Example: *I have a notebook in my desk.*

Grammar 3

Possessive of Singular and Plural Nouns

A. Fill in the blanks with possessive nouns.

1. (my mother)   This is _____*my mother's*_____ computer.

2. (Anna)   These are _____ folders.

3. (my brother)   Those are _____ pencils.

4. (Mrs. Smith)   That is _____ calculator.

5. (Thomas)   Those are _____ pens.

B. Rewrite the sentences. Use possessive nouns.

1. The girls have big umbrellas.   ⟶   ____*The girls' umbrellas*____ are big.

2. My brother has a blue backpack.   ⟶   _____ is blue.

3. Mr. Gomez has new students.   ⟶   _____ are new.

4. The students have the same schedules.   ⟶   _____ are the same.

5. Carmen has a pretty pen.   ⟶   _____ is pretty.

C. Write sentences using possessive nouns. Use the words in parentheses.

1. (my friend) *My friend's dog is black.* _____

2. (Mr. Sanchez) _____

3. (The students) _____

Reading

A. Read "Carlos's Backpack" on Student Book pages 44–45. Then answer the questions. Circle the letter of the correct answer.

1. What's Carlos's problem?

    a. He doesn't have his backpack.

    b. He has his backpack.

2. What's in his backpack?

    a. He has three books and a wallet.

    b. He has three folders, some pencils, two pens, and a wallet.

3. What does Carlos have in his wallet?

    a. He has eight dollars. **b.** He has ten dollars.

4. Does Mr. Gomez have Carlos's wallet?

    a. Yes, he does.   **b.** No, he doesn't.

5. Does Carmen have Carlos's wallet?

    a. Yes, she does.   **b.** No, she doesn't.

B. Complete each sentence. Use a word from the box.

| asks   says   problem   right   again |

1. Mr. Gomez asks Carlos, "What's in your backpack?" Then he asks

    _____, "What's in your backpack?"

2. Carlos _____, "I'm not okay."

3. Carlos has a _____. He doesn't have his backpack.

4. Mr. Gomez _____ Carlos, "What's in your wallet?"

5. Mr. Gomez says, "This is your sister's wallet." Carlos says, "Mr. Gomez, you're

    _____."

Writing

BEFORE YOU WRITE

A. Read the paragraph.

> This is my room. That is my bed. That is my desk. Those are my pens and pencils. That is my backpack. Those are my notebooks. That is my mother's calculator. That is my wallet. I have three dollars in my wallet. That is my bookcase. Those are my books. That is my cat. My cat's name is Sam.

B. Read the *Before I Write* checklist. Make notes on the lines below.

Before I Write

▶ Study the model.

▶ Think about things in my room.

▶ Make notes about my room.

1. Furniture (bed, desk, bookcase, table): _____

2. Things for school (pens, notebooks, erasers): _____

3. Other things in my room (books, wallet, pet): _____

Writing

WRITE THIS!

Read the *While I Write* checklist. Look at your notes from Exercise B and write your paragraph.

While I Write

▶ Indent the first line of the paragraph. Use capitals and periods.
  This is my room.
▶ Use *this*, *that*, *these*, or *those*. Use *is* or *are* correctly.
  That is my mother's calculator.
  Those are my pens.
▶ Use possessives (say who the things belong to).
  Those are my books.
  That is my mother's calculator.

AFTER YOU WRITE

A. Read the *After I Write* checklist. Make corrections to your paragraph above.

After I Write

▶ Did I indent the first line of the paragraph? Did I use capitals and periods?

▶ Did I use *this*, *that*, *these*, or *those*? Did I use *is* and *are* correctly?

▶ Did I say who the things belong to?

B. Make a final copy of your paragraph in your notebook.

Chapter 4

Where's the gym?

LISTENING AND READING

Read "Lost at School" on Student Book pages 50–51.
Write *True* or *False* for each statement.

1. The gym is next to Mr. Gomez's class. _____*False*_____

2. The cafeteria is downstairs. _____

3. Pablo says he is lost. _____

4. Pablo and Liliana have P.E. together. _____

5. Pablo has science with Samir. _____

6. There are three gyms in the school. _____

VOCABULARY

Complete each sentence. Use a word from the box.

| other   lost   next to   downstairs   cafeteria |

1. The school has three gyms. Two are _____.

2. Where's the gym? I'm _____.

3. You have lunch now. Go to the _____.

4. Liliana has P.E. in one gym. Pablo has P.E. in the _____ gym.

5. Mr. Gomez's class is _____ the stairs.

Grammar 1

Prepositions of Location: *in, on, under, next to*

A. Match each sentence with a picture. Write the letter on the line.

a   b   c   d

1. _c_ The cat is in the box.   **3.** ___ The cat is on the box.

2. ___ The cat is under the box.   **4.** ___ The cat is next to the box.

B. Write sentences about things you see in the picture. Use prepositions of location.

1. (notebooks)   *The notebooks are next to the cup.* _____

2. (backpack)   _____

3. (pencils)   _____

4. (book)   _____

5. (binder)   _____

C. Find things in your room. In your notebook, write three sentences about the location of those items. Use *in, on, under,* or *next to.*

Example: *My shoes are under the bed.*

Grammar 2

Where Questions with *be*

A. Fill in the blanks. For the questions, use *Where am*, *Where's*, or *Where are*.
For the answers, use contractions.

1. **A:** _____*Where's*_____ Liliana?   **B:** _____*She's*_____ in the cafeteria.

2. **A:** _____ Mei and Bic?   **B:** _____ in the library.

3. **A:** _____ Pablo?   **B:** _____ in the computer room.

4. **A:** _____ I?   **B:** _____ in the office.

5. **A:** _____ we?   **B:** _____ in room 212.

6. **A:** _____ you?   **B:** _____ in the music room.

B. Look at the picture. Write *Where* questions with *be*. Use *Where's* or *Where are*. Then write answers with *in, next to,* and *across from*. Use contractions.

1. **A:** (Tom) _____*Where's Tom?*_____

   B: _____*He's in*_____ the computer room.

2. **A:** (cafeteria) _____

   B: _____ Room 205.

3. **A:** (Sam and Chen) _____

   B: _____ the cafeteria.

4. **A:** (Robert) _____

   B: _____ the music room.

5. **A:** (library) _____

   B: _____ the music room.

6. **A:** (music room) _____

   B: _____ Room 205.

C. Look at the picture again. In your notebook, write five questions and answers
about the picture.

Example: **A:** _*Where's the computer room?*_   **B:** _*It's next to the library.*_

Word Study

Consonant Sounds: /ch/ as in *lunch* and /sh/ as in *English*

A. Look at the pictures and sound out the words. Fill in the blanks with *ch* or *sh*.

1. fi__*sh*__   **2.** ben_____   **3.** _____ip   **4.** _____in

5. di_____   **6.** lun_____   **7.** in_____   **8.** _____op

B. Look at the pictures. Fill in the blanks. Use *ch* or *sh*.

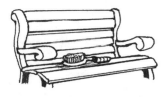

1. Do fi__*sh*__ have __*ch*__ins?

2. The hairbru_____ is on the ben_____.

3. We have lun_____ on the _____ip.

Name _____ Date _____

Grammar 3

There is and *There are*

A. Fill in the blanks with *There is* or *There are*.

1. _____*There is*_____ a new student in our class.
   (There is / There are)

2. _____ some folders on the teacher's desk.
   (There is / There are)

3. _____ twenty books in the box.
   (There is / There are)

4. _____ a table next to the door.
   (There is / There are)

5. _____ two computers on the table.
   (There is / There are)

B. Look at the picture. Write sentences about the things in the picture. Use *There's* or *There are* and *a* or *some*. Tell about location with *in*, *on*, and *next to*.

1. (books) ___*There are some books on the bed.*_____

2. (computer) _____

3. (pencils) _____

4. (desk) _____

5. (toy ship) _____

C. Write two sentences about your room at home.

Example: ___*There's a big bookcase next to my bed.*___

Reading

A. Read "I Love School!" on Student Book pages 56–57. Then answer the questions. Circle the letter of the correct answer.

1. Where's Liliana from?

    a. She's from Peru.   **b.** She's from Mexico.

2. Is she a student at Washington School?

    a. Yes, she is.   **b.** No, she isn't.

3. Where's the cafeteria?

    a. It's across from the library.

    b. It's across from one of the gyms.

4. Where are the computers?

    a. They're in the library.

    b. They're in the auditorium.

5. Does Liliana like all her classes?

    a. Yes, she does.   **b.** No, she doesn't.

B. Complete each sentence. Use a word from the box.

like	nice	a lot of	go	live

1. I come from China. Now I _____ in the United States.

2. My school is great! I _____ all my classes.

3. My teacher is very pretty and she's very _____.

4. There are _____ gyms in my school.

5. We _____ to Madison School.

Writing

BEFORE YOU WRITE

A. Read the paragraph.

I like my English class. My English class is in room 153. It's next to the computer room. My teacher is Ms. Moore. She's nice. There are books, notebooks, and pencils on her desk. There is a big table next to Ms. Moore's desk. We have two computers in our classroom. There are many desks and chairs in the classroom. My desk is next to my friend's desk. I have a lot of nice classmates.

B. Read the *Before I Write* checklist. Make notes on the lines below.

Before I Write

▶ Study the model.

▶ Think about my English classroom.

▶ Make notes about my classroom.

1. Where my classroom is (room number, next to, across from): _____

   _____

2. Things in the classroom (desks, chairs, tables, books, computers) and location
   (next to, across from, in, on): _____

   _____

3. My teacher and classmates: _____

   _____

Writing

WRITE THIS!

Read the *While I Write* checklist. Look at your notes from Exercise B and write your paragraph.

While I Write

▶ Indent the first line of the paragraph. Use capitals and periods.

   I like my English class.

▶ Use *there is* and *there are* and *have* and *has* to tell about things in your classroom.

   There are many desks and chairs in the classroom.
   We have two computers in our classroom.

▶ Use location words like *in, across from,* and *next to* to tell where things are.

   My English class is in room 153.
   My desk is next to my friend's desk.

AFTER YOU WRITE

A. Read the *After I Write* checklist. Make corrections to your paragraph above.

After I Write

▶ Did I indent the first line of the paragraph? Did I use capitals and periods?

▶ Did I use *there is* and *there are* and *has* and *have* to tell about things in my classroom?

▶ Did I use location words like *in, across from,* and *next to* to tell where things are?

B. Make a final copy of your paragraph in your notebook.

Chapter 5

What's your address?

LISTENING AND READING

Read "The Party" on Student Book pages 60–61. Then complete each sentence. Circle the letter of the correct answer.

1. Where's the party?

    a. at Liliana's house   **b.** at Carmen and Carlos's house

2. Can Samir come to the party?

    a. Yes, he can.   **b.** No, he can't.

3. What's next to Carmen and Carlos's house?

    a. a fire station   **b.** a green and white building

4. What's 555-2377?

    a. It's Carmen and Carlos's address.   **b.** It's Carmen and Carlos's phone number.

VOCABULARY

A. Look at "The Party" again. Complete the information about Carmen and Carlos.

Come to our party on Saturday!

Name: _____*Carmen*_____ and _____ Alvarez

Address: _____

Phone: _____

B. Complete each sentence. Use a word from the box.

| directions | need | come |

1. Yes, I can _____ to the party.

2. Where's your house? I need _____.

3. I also _____ a map. I don't know where Fifth Street is.

Grammar 1

What Questions with *be*

A. Complete each sentence with *What's* or *What are*.

1. _____*What's*_____ his address?

2. _____ their names?

3. _____ your favorite class?

4. _____ those?

5. _____ your best friend's name?

B. Write *what* questions to go with the answers.

1. **A:** *What's your favorite class?* _____

   B: My favorite class is art.

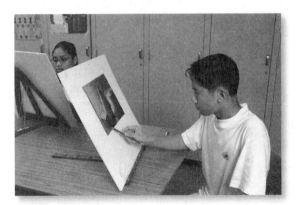

2. **A:** _____

   B: His phone number is 555-3318.

3. **A:** _____

   B: This is a map to our house.

4. **A:** _____

   B: Her brother's name is Bill.

5. **A:** _____

   B: My address is 201 Second Street.

C. In your notebook, write two *what* questions. Then write true answers.

Example: **A:** *What's your brother's name?*

   B: *My brother's name is Rodrigo.*

Grammar 2

Present Tense of Regular Verbs: Statements

A. Fill in the blanks with the correct form of the verb.

1. (need) She _____*needs*_____ a new pencil.

2. (live) You _____ in El Salvador.

3. (want) I _____ a dog.

4. (speak) They _____ Spanish.

5. (like) She _____ her teacher.

6. (ask) He _____ questions in math class.

B. Change each statement from affirmative to negative. Use *don't* and *doesn't*.

1. Laura wants a new backpack. _*Laura doesn't want a new backpack.*_____

2. Anna and Mary like tests. _____

3. I listen to music in school. _____

4. We need new notebooks. _____

5. Mrs. Perez speaks Chinese. _____

6. Julio lives in Peru. _____

Present Tense of Regular Verbs: *Yes/No* Questions

Fill in the blanks with *do*, *does*, *don't*, or *doesn't*. Then complete the short answers.

1. **A:** ____*Does*____ your brother live in New York? **B:** Yes, ___*he does*___.

2. **A:** _____ you need a new eraser? **B:** No, _____.

3. **A:** _____ your friends like music? **B:** Yes, _____.

4. **A:** _____ you want a new wallet? **B:** No, _____.

5. **A:** _____ your mother speak Spanish? **B:** Yes, _____.

6. **A:** _____ you and your sister need directions? **B:** No, _____.

Name _____ **Date** _____

Word Study

Consonant Blends as in *class*, *pretty*, and *student*

A. Look at the pictures and sound out the words. Fill in the blanks with the correct consonant blend from the box.

sw- bl- dr- cl- st- fl-

1. _____ock

2. _____ess

3. _____ack

4. _____im

5. _____um

6. _____op

7. _____ag

8. _____airs

B. Sound out the sentences. Underline words with consonant blends that come at the beginning of a word. When you find one of the words, fill in a star.

1. I love swim class. ☆☆

2. My sister has a black dress. ☆☆

3. The fire station is across from the music store. ☆☆

4. We have a flag and a clock in our classroom. ☆☆☆

C. Choose three words from Exercise A. In your notebook, write a sentence using each word.

Example: _She wants a new dress._

Grammar 3

Statements with *can*

Fill in the blanks with *can* or *can't*.

1. He _____*can*_____ play the drums. (affirmative)

2. I _____ answer the question. (negative)

3. You _____ speak English. (affirmative)

4. I _____ come to the party. (affirmative)

5. We _____ read Chinese. (negative)

6. They _____ swim. (negative)

Yes/No Questions with *can*

A. Change each statement to a question.

1. We can come to your party.   ⟶   *Can we come to your party?* _____

2. He can swim.   ⟶   _____

3. They can speak Spanish.   ⟶   _____

4. She can play the drums.   ⟶   _____

5. I can read Vietnamese.   ⟶   _____

6. You can answer the question.   ⟶   _____

B. Write *yes/no* questions about your classmates using *can*. Then write true short answers.

1. **A:** (read) *Can Miguel read Chinese?*   **B:** *No, he can't.* _____

2. **A:** (play) _____   **B:** _____

3. **A:** (speak) _____   **B:** _____

4. **A:** (come) _____   **B:** _____

5. **A:** (find) _____   **B:** _____

6. **A:** (swim) _____   **B:** _____

Reading

A. Read "Maria's Job" on Student Book pages 66–67. Then answer the questions. Circle the letter of the correct answer.

1. Can Maria go to the party?

   a. Yes, she can.   **b.** No, she can't.

2. What's Maria's job?

   a. She's a chef.   **b.** She baby-sits.

3. Does Maria like her job?

   a. Yes, she does.   **b.** No, she doesn't.

4. Does Samir have any sisters?

   a. Yes, he does.   **b.** No, he doesn't.

5. Does Carmen have a job?

   a. Yes, she does.   **b.** No, she doesn't.

B. Complete each sentence. Use a word from the box.

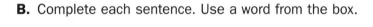

| sad | job | children | baby-sit | dance |

1. My brother has a _____. He's a chef.

2. I'm not happy today. I'm _____.

3. There's a party at our friend's house. We can _____ and have fun.

4. I _____ my little brother and sister on Saturdays.

5. My sister has two _____. She has a boy and a girl.

Writing

BEFORE YOU WRITE

A. Read the paragraph below.

> Anna Labrado is my best
> friend. She lives in Chicago. Her
> address is 453 Jackson Avenue.
> She goes to Whitehall School.
> Her favorite class is P.E. Anna
> loves music. She has a lot of
> CDs. She likes rock music. Her
> favorite singer is Gwen Stefani.

B. Read the *Before I Write* checklist. Make notes on the lines below.

Before I Write

▶ Study the model.

▶ Think about my friend.

▶ Make notes about my friend.

1. Where my friend lives (city, country, address): _____

   _____

2. Where my friend goes to school. His or her favorite class: _____

   _____

3. What music and what singers my friend likes: _____

   _____

Writing

WRITE THIS!

Read the *While I Write* checklist. Look at your notes from Exercise B and write your paragraph.

While I Write

▶ Indent the first line of the paragraph. Use capitals and periods.
   Anna Labrado is my friend.

▶ Use capital letters for cities and streets.
   She lives in Chicago.
   Her address is 453 Jackson Avenue.

▶ Use correct verb forms.
   *She **goes** to Whitehall School.*
   *Anna **loves** music.*

AFTER YOU WRITE

A. Read the *After I Write* checklist. Make corrections to your paragraph above.

After I Write

▶ Did I indent the first line of the paragraph? Did I use capitals and periods?

▶ Did I use capital letters for cities and streets?

▶ Did I use correct verb forms?

B. Make a final copy of your paragraph in your notebook.

Chapter 6

You were late yesterday.

LISTENING AND READING

Read "Late Again" on Student Book pages 70–71.
Then complete each sentence. Circle the letter
of the correct answer.

1. Is Carmen sick?

    a. Yes, she is.   **b.** No, she isn't.

2. What time does class start?

    a. It starts at ten minutes after ten.

    b. It starts at ten o'clock.

3. Where were Sophie and Carmen?

    a. They were at Carmen's house.

    b. They were in the hall.

4. Was Carmen late to class yesterday?

    a. Yes, she was.   **b.** No, she wasn't.

5. Where is Sophie from?

    a. She's from France.   **b.** She's from Haiti.

VOCABULARY

Complete each sentence. Use a word or phrase from the box.

starts	today	late	sick	take out

1. I was in the hall. I'm sorry I'm _____ for class.

2. Richard isn't at school today. He's at home. He's _____.

3. Please _____ a piece of paper. Write your name on it.

4. My science class _____ at three o'clock.

5. I was late to class yesterday. I'm sorry I'm late again _____.

Grammar 1

What Questions with do

A. Complete the questions. Fill in the blanks with *do* or *does*.

1. What _____*does*_____ Carlos need?

2. What _____ you want?

3. What other languages _____ Sophie speak?

4. What _____ they like?

5. What _____ you and Carmen have?

B. Write *What* questions with *do* or *does*.

1. **A:** _What does he like?_____

   B: He likes enchiladas.

2. **A:** _____

   B: I have ten dollars.

3. **A:** _____

   B: She wants a new CD.

4. **A:** _____

   B: I play the drums.

5. **A:** _____

   B: We need a calculator.

C. Ask a friend two *What* questions with *do* or *does*. Write the questions and answers.

Example: You: _What do you have in your backpack?_

Your friend: _I have some pencils and two notebooks._

1. You: _____

   Your friend: _____

2. You _____

   Your friend: _____

Grammar 2

What + Noun

A. Write the questions.

1. (class) What do you have next? _*What class do you have next?*_

2. (color) What do you like? _____

3. (classes) What does your friend have? _____

4. (books) What do you need for school? _____

B. Complete the dialogue. Write *What* questions using *What* + noun.

1. **A:** (school) _*What school do you go to?*_

   B: I go to Wilson School.

2. **A:** (classes) _____
   _____?

   B: I have history, math, science, art, P.E., music, and English.

3. **A:** (time) _____
   _____?

   B: My classes start at eight thirty.

4. **A:** (time) _____
   _____?

   B: I go home at three thirty.

C. Copy the questions in Exercise B into your notebook. Then write true answers.

Example: **A:** _*What school do you go to?*_
          B: _*I go to South Street School.*_

Word Study

Consonant Blends as in fi**nd**, wa**nt**, and be**st**

A. Look at the pictures and sound out the words. Fill in the blanks with the correct consonant blend from the box.

-ft	-sk	-nt	-mp	-lt	-nd

1. pla_____

2. ma_____

3. gi_____

4. ha_____

5. be_____

6. la_____

7. te_____

8. de_____

B. Look at the pictures. Write a word from Exercise A with the same final consonant blend.

ant

ask

stamp

stand

1. ___*plant*___

2. _____

3. _____

4. _____

C. Choose four words from Exercise A. In your notebook, write a sentence using each word.

Example: *I have a gift for my little sister.*

Grammar 3

Past Tense of *be*: Statements

A. Change each statement from the present tense to the past tense. Use *wasn't* or *weren't* in negative sentences.

1. You're late today. → _____*You were late*_____ yesterday.

2. I'm very silly today. → _____ yesterday.

3. The class isn't hard today. → _____ yesterday.

4. Mrs. Moore is funny today. → _____ yesterday.

5. Ted and Ann aren't in school today. → _____ yesterday.

6. You're sick today. → _____ yesterday.

B. Think about yesterday at school (or last Friday). Circle the correct form of *be* to make each sentence true for you.

1. My English teacher (was /(wasn't)) angry yesterday.

2. I (was / wasn't) late to school yesterday.

3. My best friends (were / weren't) in school yesterday.

4. My English class (was / wasn't) hard yesterday.

5. I (was / wasn't) in the library after school yesterday.

6. My friends (were / weren't) at lunch yesterday.

Past Tense of *be*: Yes/No Questions

Look at the sentences in Exercise B. Write *yes/no* questions and true short answers.
Use contractions (*wasn't, weren't*).

1. **A:** _*Was your English teacher angry yesterday?*_   **B:** _*No, she wasn't.*_

2. **A:** _____   **B:** _____

3. **A:** _____   **B:** _____

4. **A:** _____   **B:** _____

5. **A:** _____   **B:** _____

6. **A:** _____   **B:** _____

Reading

A. Read "My Journal" on Student Book pages 76–77. Then answer the questions. Circle the letter of the correct answer.

1. On Monday, Carmen was in her English class at ___.

   a. 9:55   **b.** 10:05   **c.** 10:10

2. On Monday, Carmen was in her math class at ___.

   a. 12:50   **b.** 1:00   **c.** 1:10

3. On Tuesday, Carmen was ___.

   a. early for math   **b.** early for math and   **c.** late for math
   and English   late for English   and English

4. On Tuesday, Mr. Gomez was ___.

   a. not angry   **b.** angry   **c.** late

5. Carmen needs a ___.

   a. book   **b.** pencil   **c.** watch

B. Complete each sentence. Use a word from the box.

tomorrow	bad	watch	easy	early

1. The test was not hard. It was pretty _____.

2. Mr. Gomez was angry yesterday. I was late again. It was a _____ day.

3. I don't know what time it is. I need a _____.

4. Class starts at nine o'clock. I was in class at ten to eight. I was _____.

5. Yesterday I was late for science class. Today I was late again. I know I can be on time
   _____.

Writing

BEFORE YOU WRITE

A. Read the paragraph below. Make a story. Circle one word or phrase in each set.
Then read your story.

Randy's Day

Yesterday was (a good / a bad / (an okay))
day for Randy. He was (early / on time / late)
to his (math / history / science / art / English /
P.E. / music) class. What time was he in class? He
was in class (before / after / at) ten. His teacher was
(angry / not angry). There was a test in the class.
Randy was pretty (nervous / happy / worried) about
the test. He (studied / didn't study) very hard. The test was pretty (easy /
hard) for him. After the test Randy was very (happy / worried).

B. Read the *Before I Write* checklist. Make notes on the lines below.

Before I Write

▶ Study the model.

▶ Think about the words I want to use in my story.

▶ Think about a story. Think about a friend or someone in my family.

1. My friend or family member's name: _____

2. What that person did: _____.

_____.

3. Where that person was: _____.

4. How the person felt: _____.

Writing

WRITE THIS!

Read the *While I Write* checklist. Look at your notes from Exercise B and write your paragraph.

While I Write

▶ Use describing words to tell how the person felt.
*Randy was pretty **nervous** about the test.*

▶ Use *was* or *were* to write about the past.
*The test **was** pretty hard for him.*

▶ Give details about time and place.
*He was **in class after ten**.*

_____ *Day*

AFTER YOU WRITE

A. Read the *After I Write* checklist. Make corrections to your paragraph above.

After I Write

▶ Did I use describing words to tell how the person felt?

▶ Did I use *was* or *were* to write about the past?

▶ Did I give details about time and place?

B. Make a final copy of your paragraph in your notebook.

Chapter 7

What are you doing?

LISTENING AND READING

Read "Help for Carlos" on Student Book pages 82–83.
Then answer the questions. Use complete sentences.

1. Does Carlos need help?

   _____

2. Can David help Carlos?

   _____

3. Is Carlos's mother busy?

   _____

4. Can Carolina help Carlos?

   _____

5. Is Carlos's grandmother busy?

   _____

6. Can Carlos's grandmother help him?

   _____

VOCABULARY

Read the dialogue again. Write what each person is doing. Use words from the box.

cleaning the windows	making the bed	cooking
changing a lightbulb	washing her hair	

1. (Carlos's father) _Carlos's father is changing a lightbulb._ _____

2. (Carmen) _____

3. (Carlos) _____

4. (David) _____

5. (Carolina) _____

Grammar 1

Present Continuous Tense: Statements

A. Look at the picture. Circle the words that show the activities.

cleaning the floor	playing the drums	eating a snack
changing a lightbulb	~~writing on the board~~	dancing
reading a book	(helping Mr. Green)	listening to music

B. Look at the picture in Exercise A again. Complete the sentences. Tell what the people are doing. Use words from the box in Exercise A.

1. Renee _is helping Mr. Green._

4. Anna _____

2. Mr. Green _____

5. Manuel and Lee _____

3. Abdul _____

6. Flavio _____

C. Rewrite the sentences. Use *isn't* and *aren't*.

1. She's not cleaning the table.   ⟶   _She isn't cleaning the table._

2. He's not changing a lightbulb.   ⟶   _____

3. We're not writing in our notebooks.   ⟶   _____

4. You're not reading a book.   ⟶   _____

5. They're not making enchiladas.   ⟶   _____

Grammar 2

Present Continuous Tense: *What* Questions

A. Complete the questions. Write *What's* or *What are* in the blanks.

1. _____*What's*_____ she studying?

2. _____ they cooking?

3. _____ he eating?

4. _____ you writing?

5. _____ it doing?

6. _____ we reading?

B. Read each answer. Write the question it responds to. Use pronouns.

1. Mei and Sophie are eating lunch.   *What are they eating?* _____

2. Mr. Gomez is writing the answers.   _____

3. Maria is studying math.   _____

4. Pablo and Kim are making cookies.   _____

Present Continuous Tense: *Yes/No* Questions

Look at the pictures. Write the answers. Say what the people are doing.

Is Lee writing a letter?

1. *No, he isn't. He's studying math.* _____

Is Jen dancing?

2. _____

_____

Are Mrs. Chan and Mee washing the dishes?

3. _____

_____

Word Study

Long Vowel Sounds /ā/ as in *came*, /ī/ as in *like*, /ō/ as in *close*, /yo͞o/ as in *use*

A. Look at the pictures and sound out the words. Fill in the blanks with *a, i, o,* or *u.*

1. n___se

2. b___ke

3. c___te

4. c___ke

5. c___be

6. n___me

7. ph___ne

8. wr___te

B. Sound out the sentences. Circle words with the long vowel sounds /ā/, /ī/, /ō/, or /yo͞o/. When you find one of the words, fill in a star.

1. He likes ice cubes in his drink.   ☆☆☆

2. She has a cute nose.   ☆☆

3. Open the phone book to the first page.   ☆☆☆

4. We like cake and ice cream.   ☆☆☆

C. Choose three words from Exercise A. In your notebook, write a sentence using each word.

Example: *I'm making a cake for my sister's birthday.*

Grammar 3

Object Pronouns

A. Underline the objects in the sentences. Then rewrite the sentences using object pronouns.

1. I'm helping <u>Carlos and his grandmother</u>. ⟶ *I'm helping them.*

2. She's helping Carlos. ⟶ _____

3. They're burning the enchiladas. ⟶ _____

4. He's asking his mother. ⟶ _____

5. We're making a cake. ⟶ _____

6. She's cooking with Carlos and me. ⟶ _____

7. When is your mother baking a cake? ⟶ _____

8. Where are you going with your sister? ⟶ _____

9. What's he making for you and your friend? ⟶ _____

B. Circle the subjects and underline the objects in the sentences. Then complete the answers using object pronouns.

1. Are (you) drying <u>the dishes?</u>

   Yes, *I'm drying them.* _____

2. Is your mother reading this book?

   Yes, _____

3. Are your brother and sister eating the cookies?

   Yes, _____

4. Is your brother asking your father?

   Yes, _____

5. Are your sisters helping you and your brother?

   Yes, _____

6. Are you studying with Bob and Carlos?

   Yes, _____

7. Are you cleaning your room?

   Yes, _____

8. Are you eating with your grandmother?

   Yes, _____

Reading

A. Read "Getting Ready" on Student Book pages 88–89. Then match each sentence in the left-hand column with a sentence from the right-hand column. Write the letter on the line.

1. _b_ The family is getting ready for a party.   **a.** He is in the living room.

2. ____ The mother is sweeping the floor.   **b.** They are in the house.

3. ____ The brother is washing the windows.   **c.** She is in the entranceway.

4. ____ The grandmother is cooking enchiladas.   **d.** She is in the kitchen.

5. ____ The sister is washing her hair.   **e.** She is in the bathroom.

B. Complete the sentences about the reading. Use words from the box.

turning	knocking	helping	cool	later	get ready

1. Carmen and Carlos are angry. Carolina isn't _____ the family.

2. Carolina is washing her hair. Mother says Carolina can help _____.

3. Carlos and Carmen need time to _____.

4. At four o'clock, Carmen and Carlos are _____ on the bathroom door.

5. Carolina is worried. Her hair is _____ blue.

6. Carlos says Carolina's hair is _____. He wants blue hair, too.

Writing

BEFORE YOU WRITE

A. Read the paragraph below.

> It is seven o'clock. Everyone in my family is busy. My mother, brother, and father are in the kitchen. My father is cooking dinner. My mother is washing the dishes and my brother is drying them. My grandmother is in the living room. She is watching TV and she is talking on the phone. My sister is cleaning her bedroom. She's sweeping her floor for the third time! She loves to clean her room! I am in my bedroom. I am listening to music and I am writing this paragraph now.

B. Read the *Before I Write* checklist. Make notes on the lines below.

Before I Write
▶ Study the model.
▶ Think about about a time of day at my house (for example, seven o'clock).
▶ Make notes about where each person in my family is and what each person is doing.

1. Where each person is at _____ o'clock: _____

_____

_____

2. What each person is doing at that time:_____

_____

_____

Writing

WRITE THIS!

Read the *While I Write* checklist. Look at your notes from Exercise B and write your paragraph.

While I Write

▶ Use the present continuous to write about what is happening.

*My father **is cooking** dinner.*

▶ Use the simple present to say where someone is, or how someone is.

*Everyone in my family **is** busy.*
*My mother, brother, and father **are** in the kitchen.*

▶ Use subject and object pronouns (*he, she, they,* or *him, her, them*) in place of nouns.

***She** loves to clean her room!*
*My mother is washing dishes and my brother is drying **them**.*

AFTER YOU WRITE

A. Read the *After I Write* checklist. Make corrections to your paragraph above.

After I Write

▶ Did I use the present continuous to write about what is happening?

▶ Did I use the simple present to say where someone is, or how someone is?

▶ Did I use pronouns like *he, she, they,* or *him, her, them* in place of nouns?

B. Make a final copy of your paragraph in your notebook.

Chapter 8

I have to work.

LISTENING AND READING

Read "The Telephone Calls" on Student Book pages 92–93.
Then read the questions. Circle the letter of the correct answer.

1. When is Carmen and Carlos's party?

   a. It's tomorrow.　　**(b.)** It's tonight.　　**c.** It was yesterday.

2. What does Maria have to do?

   a. She has to work.　　**b.** She has to baby-sit.　　**c.** Both a and b.

3. Who wants to go to the party with Maria?

   a. Pablo does.　　**b.** Samir does.　　**c.** Both a and b.

4. Does Maria want to go to the party?

   a. Yes, she does.　　**b.** No, she doesn't.　　**c.** We don't know.

5. Who can baby-sit for Maria?

   a. Her mother can.　　**b.** Paco can.　　**c.** Both a and b.

6. Who does Maria have to go to the party with?

   a. She has to go with Pablo.　　**b.** She has to go with Paco.　　**c.** Both a and b.

VOCABULARY

Complete the telephone conversation. Use words from the box.

tonight	another	work	too bad	go out	would

Luz: Hello.

Jason: Hi, Luz. This is Jason. Would you like to go out (1) _____*tonight*_____?

Luz: I'm sorry, I can't (2) _____ tonight.

　　　I have to (3) _____.

Jason: That's (4) _____. (5) _____ you like

　　　to go out (6) _____ night?

Luz: Yes, Jason. Thank you.

Grammar 1

Simple Present Tense and Present Continuous Tense

A. Complete the sentences. Fill in the blanks with the simple present or present continuous form of the verb.

1. I _____*am talking*_____ on the phone now. (talk)

2. My mother _____*makes*_____ my lunch every day. (make)

3. I cannot go out now. I _____. (study)

4. My grandfather _____ TV every night after dinner. (watch)

5. Oh, no! Turn off the stove now! You _____ the cookies! (burn)

6. My sister cannot come to the phone. She _____ her hair now. (wash)

7. My mother and father _____ every Saturday night. (go out)

8. I _____ my grandmother every Sunday. (call)

9. I can play after dinner. I _____ my homework right now. (do)

B. Complete the telephone dialogue. Fill in the blanks with *make* in the simple present or present continuous.

(The telephone rings.)

A: What are you doing now?

B: I **(1)** *am making* dinner.

A: Oh? **(2)** _____ you

_____ dinner every night?

B: I **(3)** _____ dinner when my mother has to work.

A: What **(4)** _____ you _____ tonight?

B: I **(5)** _____ chili.

A: **(6)** _____ you _____ chili a lot?

B: Yes, I do. I love chili. I **(7)** _____ chili every Monday.

A: Can I come over and help you **(8)** _____ dinner?

B: Sure, you can come over. We'll **(9)** _____ dinner together.

Grammar 2

Sentences with *like*, *have*, and *want* + Infinitive

A. Complete the sentences. Fill in the blanks with the correct form of the verb.

1. My sister _____ *likes* _____ to play soccer. (like)

2. I _____ to clean the house. (have)

3. My best friend _____ to go out tonight. (want)

4. My brother _____ to baby-sit my sister. (have)

5. My friends _____ to come to my house. (want)

6. My mother and grandmother _____ to talk on the phone. (like)

B. Change each statement from affirmative to negative. Use *don't* and *doesn't*.

1. My brother has to work today. *My brother doesn't have to work today.* _____

2. I like to write letters. _____

3. My father likes to dance. _____

4. My sisters want to wash the dishes. _____

5. My friends have to study tonight. _____

C. In your notebook, write three true affirmative statements about yourself. Use *like*, *want*, and *have* + infinitive. You can use words from the box or your own ideas.

cook dinner	clean my bedroom	talk on the phone	baby-sit
study	read	watch TV	listen to music
dance	wash the dishes	go to parties	go out

Example: *I like to watch TV.*

D. In your notebook, write three true negative statements about yourself. Use *like*, *have*, and *want* + infinitive. You can use words from the box in Exercise C or your own ideas.

Example: *I don't like to clean my bedroom.*

Word Study

Long Vowel Sound: /ā/ as in *take*

A. Look at the pictures and sound out the words. Fill in the blanks with *a___e*, *ai*, or *ay*.

1. r_____n

2. pl_____

3. m_____l

4. g___m___

5. s_____

6. tr_____n

7. c___k___

8. p___g___

B. Read the story aloud. Circle the words with the long vowel sound /ā/.

I like to visit my grandmother. She lives next to a big lake. You can ride a train all around the lake. Sometimes my grandmother makes lunch for us. We eat our lunch by the lake, we play games, and we always ride on the train. It's a lot of fun!

Grammar 3

What Questions with *like, have,* and *want* + Infinitive

Look at the chart. Complete the dialogues. Write *what* questions and answers.

	like	have	want
Kim	play soccer	do homework	visit his grandmother
Marco	ride his bike	clean his room	go to the movies
Ken	play soccer	take out the garbage	go to the movies

1. A: *What does Marco like to do?*

   B: *He likes to ride his bike.*

2. A: *What do Marco and Ken want to do?*

   B: *They want to go to the movies.*

3. A: _____

   B: *He has to clean his room.*

4. A: *What does Kim want to do?*

   B: _____

5. A: *What do Kim and Ken like to do?*

   B: _____

6. A: _____

   B: *He has to do homework.*

Yes/No Questions with *like, have,* and *want* + Infinitive

Answer the questions.

1. Do you like to clean your room? _____

2. Do your friends have to do homework on Saturday? _____

3. Do you have to wash the dishes at your house? _____

4. Do your friends like to watch TV? _____

5. Do you want to go to the movies this Saturday? _____

6. Does your family like to go out to dinner? _____

Reading

A. Read "Maria" on Student Book pages 98–99.
Then answer the questions. Use complete sentences.

1. Does Maria sometimes feel homesick?

   _____

2. Who does Maria miss in El Salvador?

   _____

3. What does Maria do after her homework?

   _____

4. Does she want to show her art to other people?

   _____

5. What does Maria do on Saturday nights?

   _____

B. Fill in the blanks with information from the reading.

Name: _Maria Lopez_	**Age:** _____ years old
Country: lives in _____ / comes from _____	
School: _Washington School_	**Likes to:** _____ and _____

C. Complete each sentence. Use a word from the box.

homesick	feel	homework	sometimes	draw

1. I'm excited. Today is my birthday. I _____ happy.

2. I don't have any _____, so I can play after school.

3. I like to _____ pictures with my pencil in my notebook.

4. Sometimes I feel _____. I miss my friends in Mexico.

5. I speak English most of the time at home. But _____ I speak Spanish.

Writing

BEFORE YOU WRITE

A. Read the paragraph below.

> I like to go out on weekends. Sometimes my friends and I go shopping. Sometimes we go to the movies. And sometimes we play sports. We love to play soccer. Sometimes my mother has to work on weekends. Then I have to baby-sit my little brother. I can't see my friends. But I can talk to my friends on the phone. And sometimes a friend comes over to my house. We talk and play video games. On Sundays I have to do my homework.

B. Read the *Before I Write* checklist. Make notes on the lines below.

Before I Write

▶ Study the model.

▶ Think about what I do on weekends.

▶ Make notes about what I do on weekends.

1. What I like to do on weekends:

_____

2. What I sometimes do on weekends:

_____

3. What I sometimes have to do on weekends:

_____

Writing

WRITE THIS!

Read the *While I Write* checklist. Look at your notes from Exercise B and write your paragraph.

While I Write

▶ Use *like* + infinitive to tell what activities I like to do.
   *I **like to go** out on weekends.*

▶ Use the simple present to tell what I sometimes do.
   *Sometimes my friends and I **go** shopping.*

▶ Use *have* + infinitive to tell what I need to do.
   *On Sundays I **have to do** my homework.*

AFTER YOU WRITE

A. Read the *After I Write* checklist. Make corrections to your paragraph above.

After I Write

▶ Did I use *like* + infinitive to tell what activities I like to do?

▶ Did I use the simple present to tell what I sometimes do?

▶ Did I use *have* + infinitive to tell what I need to do?

B. Make a final copy of your paragraph in your notebook.

Chapter 9

You came to our party!

LISTENING AND READING

Read "Maria and Paco" on Student Book pages 102–103.
Then answer the questions. Write complete sentences.

Happy Birthday Carmen and Carlos

1. How old are Carmen and Carlos?

   _____

2. What are Carmen and Carlos?

   _____

3. Do Carlos, Samir, and Pablo know Paco?

   _____

4. Who does Paco want to dance with?

   _____

5. Who do Carlos, Pablo, and Samir want to dance with?

   _____

VOCABULARY

Complete each sentence. Use a word from the box.

introduce	twins	both	wrong	let's

1. What do you want to do? I know! _____ go to the park.

2. My friend and I have the same birthday. We are _____ fifteen years old.

3. Juan said the party was on Saturday. I know the party was on Sunday.

   Juan was _____.

4. Hey, Lee. I want to _____ you to Sam. Sam, this is Lee.

   Lee, this is Sam.

5. Tom and Tim are brothers. They're both sixteen and they have the same

   birthday. They're _____.

Grammar 1

Past Tense of Regular Verbs: Affirmative Statements

A. Write the past tense form.

1. laugh ⟶ *laughed*

2. dance ⟶ _____

3. want ⟶ _____

4. ask ⟶ _____

5. like ⟶ _____

6. arrive ⟶ _____

7. talk ⟶ _____

8. wash ⟶ _____

9. study ⟶ _____

10. cook ⟶ _____

11. change ⟶ _____

12. play ⟶ _____

13. help ⟶ _____

14. need ⟶ _____

B. Change the sentences to the past tense. Add *yesterday*.

1. We clean the house.

   We cleaned the house yesterday.

2. We listen to music.

   _____

3. He watches TV.

   _____

4. They play soccer.

   _____

5. She studies history.

   _____

C. In your notebook, write three sentences about what you did yesterday. Use verbs from Exercise A.

Example: *I helped my father yesterday.*

Grammar 2

Past Tense of Irregular Verbs: Affirmative Statements

A. Write the past tense form.

1. come ⟶ _____   7. write ⟶ _____

2. eat ⟶ _____   8. make ⟶ _____

3. say ⟶ _____   9. do ⟶ _____

4. sing ⟶ _____   10. go ⟶ _____

5. teach ⟶ _____   11. know ⟶ _____

6. read ⟶ _____   12. have ⟶ _____

B. Change the sentences to the past tense. Use the words in parentheses.

1. We <u>eat</u> lunch at twelve o'clock <u>every day</u>. (yesterday)

   We ate lunch at twelve o'clock yesterday.

2. I <u>go</u> to the movies <u>every weekend</u>. (last Saturday)

   _____

3. I <u>sing</u> in the bathroom <u>every night</u>. (last night)

   _____

4. I <u>have</u> breakfast at seven o'clock <u>every day</u>. (yesterday)

   _____

5. My teacher <u>says</u> "Good Morning!" <u>every morning</u>. (this morning)

   _____

6. Ms. Smith <u>teaches</u> math <u>every day</u>. (yesterday)

   _____

C. In your notebook, write three past tense sentences. Use words from Exercise A.

Example: *My grandmother made cookies yesterday.*

Word Study

Long Vowel Sound: /ē/ as in *me*

A. Look at the pictures and sound out the words. Fill in the blanks with *e*, *ea*, *ee*, *y*, or *ie*.

1. m_____t

2. cit___

3. f_____ld

4. m___

5. bab___

6. cl_____n

7. r_____d

8. tr_____

B. Sound out the sentences. Circle the words with the long vowel sound /ē/.
When you find one of the words, fill in a star.

1. We are so happy to see you. ☆☆☆

2. There are a lot of trees in this city. ☆☆

3. I'm reading a book about feet. ☆☆

4. He asked me to clean the field. ☆☆☆☆

C. Choose three words from Exercise A. In your notebook, write a sentence using each word.

Example: *The baby is happy.*

Grammar 3

Past Tense: Negative Statements

A. Change the sentences in the left-hand column from affirmative to negative. Then match the sentences in the left-hand column with sentences in the right-hand column.

               didn't go

1. _c_ Maria ~~went~~ to the movies on Saturday.   **a.** She ate pizza.

2. ___ Carmen ate ice cream at the party.   **b.** It was at Carlos and Carmen's house.

3. ___ Carlos and Samir asked Carmen to dance.   **c.** She went to Carlos's party.

4. ___ Pablo played the drums.   **d.** She talked to Pablo.

5. ___ The party was at Maria's house.   **e.** He played his guitar.

6. ___ Liliana talked to Paco.   **f.** They asked Maria to dance.

B. In your notebook, write five sentences about what you, your family, and friends didn't do in the past. Use *yesterday*, *last night*, *last week*, *on Saturday*, or *on Sunday*.

Example: *My mother didn't make enchiladas for me last night.*

Past Tense: *Yes/No* Questions

Write *yes/no* questions for these statements.

1. I didn't eat ice cream yesterday.   ⟶   *Did you eat ice cream yesterday?*

2. I didn't do homework last night.   ⟶   _____

3. I went out with my friends on Saturday.   ⟶   _____

4. I cleaned my room this morning.   ⟶   _____

5. I didn't watch TV Sunday morning.   ⟶   _____

6. I didn't help my mother on Sunday.   ⟶   _____

Reading

A. Read "A Fun Party" on Student Book pages 108–109.
Then answer the questions. Use complete sentences.

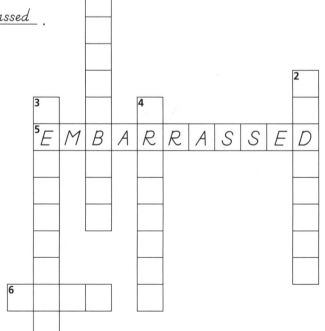

1. Did everybody at the party have fun?

_____

2. Who wrote Pablo's song?

_____

3. Who did the girls and boys talk about?

_____

4. Did the boys like Paco?

_____

5. What time did Paco and Maria have to go home?

_____

B. Complete each sentence. Use a word from the box. Then write the answers in the puzzle.

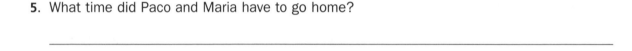

| midnight | promised | delicious | everybody | cute | embarrassed |

ACROSS

5. Her hair turned blue. She was _embarrassed_ .

6. She likes that boy a lot.

She thinks he's _____.

DOWN

1. All my friends came to the party.

_____ had a good time.

2. It's eleven fifty at night.

It's almost _____.

3. I loved the cake.

It was _____!

4. I have to go home now.

I _____ my mother.

Writing

BEFORE YOU WRITE

A. Read the paragraph below.

> Yesterday I went to school. I arrived at school at seven forty-five. I had math, history, and English classes in the morning. After lunch I had P.E., music, and science. School was over at three o'clock. I got home at three thirty and watched TV. Then I did my homework. We ate dinner at seven o'clock. I didn't eat a lot. After dinner I went to my bedroom and listened to music. My friend Manuel called. After an hour my mother told me to get off the phone. She said dessert was ready. Then we all ate ice cream and talked. I went to bed at ten o'clock. It was a nice day.

B. Read the *Before I Write* checklist. Make notes on the lines below.

Before I Write

▶ Study the model.

▶ Think about what I did yesterday. If yesterday was Saturday or Sunday, think about what I did Friday.

▶ Make notes about what I did yesterday or Friday.

1. What time I arrived at school and what classes I had:

   _____

2. What time I got home and what I did before dinner:

   _____

3. What time I ate dinner and what I did before going to bed:

   _____

Writing

WRITE THIS!

Read the *While I Write* checklist. Look at your notes from Exercise B and write your paragraph.

While I Write

▶ Use the past tense form of verbs to write about the past.
   *Yesterday I **went** to school.*

▶ Use *did* and *didn't* to say what you did and didn't do.
   *I **did** my homework.*
   *I **didn't eat** a lot.*

▶ Use time expressions to say when you did something.
   *I arrived at school at **seven forty-five**.*

▶ Use words like *then* and *after* to say what you did next.
   ***Then** we all ate ice cream and talked.*

AFTER YOU WRITE

A. Read the *After I Write* checklist. Make corrections to your paragraph above.

After I Write

▶ Did I use the past tense form of verbs to write about the past?

▶ Did I use *did* and *didn't* to say what I did and didn't do?

▶ Did I use time expressions to say when I did something?

▶ Did I use words like *then* and *after* to say what I did next?

B. Make a final copy of your paragraph in your notebook.

Chapter 10

How much is it?

LISTENING AND READING

Read "Pablo's New Clothes" on Student Book pages 114–115. Then answer the questions. Use complete sentences.

1. What clothes does Pablo need?

   _____

2. Why does Pablo need new clothes?

   _____

3. Does Pablo have a girlfriend?

   _____

4. What color shirt does Pablo want?

   _____

5. What does Pablo need to try on?

   _____

VOCABULARY

Complete each sentence. Use a word from the box.

| girlfriend | clothes | secret | expensive | try on |

1. These jeans are $99.99. They're really _____!

2. Can you wait? I need to _____ this jacket.

3. He likes Sara a lot. He wants her to be his _____.

4. I need some new _____. I need a shirt, pants, and a jacket.

5. Don't ask! I can't tell you. It's a _____.

Grammar 1

Information Questions with *be*: Present Tense

Complete the sentences. Use the present-tense form of *be* and a word from the box.

who	what	when	where	why	how

1. _____*What is*_____ your secret?

2. _____ the cafeteria?

3. _____ your birthday?

4. _____ your English teacher this year?

5. _____ he sitting on the floor?

6. _____ the weather?

Information Questions with *be*: Past Tense

A. Complete the dialogue. Use the past-tense form of *be* and question words from the box above.

1. **A:** _____*Where were*_____ you on Monday and Tuesday?

   B: I was at home.

2. **A:** _____ you at home?

   B: I was home because I was sick.

3. **A:** _____ Carlos's party?

   B: It was last Saturday afternoon.

4. **A:** _____ at the party?

   B: Carmen, Maria, Pablo, and his family were at the party.

5. **A:** _____ the English test?

   B: It was very hard.

6. **A:** _____ the questions?

   B: I can't tell you that!

B. In your notebook, write five information questions with *be*. You can use the present or past-tense form of *be*. Use a different question word in each question.

Example: *How are you today?*

Grammar 2

Information Questions with *do*: Present Tense

A. Match each question in the left-hand column with an answer in the right-hand column. Write the letter on the line.

1. _*d*_ What do you do on Saturday?   **a.** I go home after the game.

2. ___ Who do you play soccer with?   **b.** I play at the park.

3. ___ Where do you do play?   **c.** I play in the morning.

4. ___ When do you play?   **d.** I play soccer on Saturday.

5. ___ Why do you play soccer?   **e.** I play soccer because it's fun.

6. ___ What do you do after the game?   **f.** I play with my friends.

B. Write a question for each answer.

1. _*What does your sister do on Saturday?*_   My sister goes shopping on Saturday.

2. _____   She goes to Dupont Mall.

3. _____   She goes there because it's fun.

4. _____   She goes with me.

5. _____   We go shopping on Saturday.

6. _____   We buy books and clothes.

Information Questions with *do*: Past Tense

Change the questions from the present to the past.

1. How do they look?   _*How did they look?*_ _____

2. How much does it cost?   _____

3. When does the movie start?   _____

4. What do you want to do?   _____

5. Who do you play baseball with?   _____

6. Where does your friend go shopping?   _____

Word Study

Long Vowel Sound: /ī/ as in *pie*

A. Look at the pictures and sound out the words. Fill in the blanks with *i___e, y, i, ie,* or *igh*.

1. p_____   **2.** n___n___   **3.** ch___ld   **4.** cr___

5. l_____t   **6.** dr___   **7.** n_____t   **8.** b___k___

B. Sound out the words in each column. Check "yes" if all the words have the long vowel sound /ī/. Check "no" if they do not.

1. ride	**2.** why	**3.** right	**4.** fire
bike	child	shirt	time
night	cry	size	nine
☐ yes ☐ no	☐ yes ☐ no	☐ yes ☐ no	☐ yes ☐ no

C. Choose three words from Exercise A. In your notebook, write a sentence using each word.

Example: *That's my bike.*

Grammar 3

Questions with *how much*

A. Fill in the blanks with *is*, *are*, *do*, or *does*.

1. How much _____*does*_____ this dress cost?

2. How much _____ these jeans cost?

3. How much _____ those shoes?

4. How much _____ this hat cost?

5. How much _____ that belt?

6. How much _____ these socks cost?

7. How much _____ this skirt?

B. Look at the pictures. Write questions and answers about the prices of the items. For each question, use the correct form of the verb in parentheses. Write the prices.

1. **A:** _How much do these shoes cost?_____ (do)

   B: _They're $32.50._____

$32.50

$16.99

2. **A:** _How much is this shirt?_____ (be)

   B: _It's $16.99._____

3. **A:** _____ (be)

   B: _____

$24.50

4. **A:** _____ (do)

   B: _____

$49.95

5. **A:** _____ (be)

   B: _____

$12.99

6. **A:** _____ (be)

   B: _____

$3.25

Name _____ Date _____

Reading

A. Read "A Forty-Dollar Dress" on Student Book pages 120–121. Then answer the questions.

1. What did Maria want?

   _____

2. How much money did Maria have?

   _____

3. Why did the girls have to be at the fountain at six?

   _____

B. Complete each sentence. Use a word from the box. Write the answers in the puzzle.

| found | price tag | supermarket | suddenly | only | shopping | color |

ACROSS

2. Maria loved the dress, but the _____ didn't look good on her.

4. Carmen _____ a very nice dress, but it cost a hundred and fifty dollars!

5. The _____ said the jacket cost $150.

7. All the girls were having fun, but _____ Mei said she had to go.

DOWN

1. Maria, Carmen, and Mei went _____ for some new clothes.

3. After the girls went shopping, they went to the _____ for Mei's grandmother.

6. Maria liked the dress Carmen showed her, but she _____ had forty dollars.

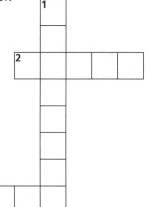

Writing

BEFORE YOU WRITE

A. Read the paragraph below.

> My favorite shirt is blue and white. It's very cool. I wear it almost every week. Blue is a good color for me. I'm wearing it now! My mother bought it for me last year. I think it was only about ten dollars. She bought it in a department store in Shanghai, China. You can buy a lot of clothes in China. They're very nice and they aren't expensive.

B. Read the *Before I Write* checklist. Make notes on the lines below.

Before I Write

▶ Study the model.

▶ Think about my favorite clothing item.

▶ Make notes about my favorite clothing item.

1. What color it is:

_____

2. Why I like it:

_____

3. Where I can buy it:

_____

4. How much it costs:

_____

5. When I wear it:

_____

Writing

WRITE THIS!

Read the *While I Write* checklist. Look at your notes from Exercise B and write your paragraph.

While I Write

▶ Use the present tense to write about what is true now.
   *My favorite shirt **is** blue and white.*

▶ Use the past tense to write about what happened in the past.
   *She **bought** it in a department store in Shanghai, China.*

▶ Use *it* for singular clothing items, and *they/them* for plural items.
   *(a shirt) **It's** very cool.*
   *(clothes) **They're** very nice.*

AFTER YOU WRITE

A. Read the *After I Write* checklist. Make corrections to your paragraph above.

After I Write

▶ Did I use the present tense to write about what's true now?

▶ Did I use the past tense to write about what happened in the past?

▶ Did I use *it* for singular clothing items, and *they/them* for plural items?

B. Make a final copy of your paragraph in your notebook.

Chapter 11

She needs some lettuce.

LISTENING AND READING

Read "I'm So Hungry" on Student Book pages 124–125.
Then answer the questions. Use complete sentences.

1. Does Mei's grandmother need any lettuce?

_____

2. How many eggs does Mei's grandmother need?

_____

3. Why does Carmen want to eat some crackers?

_____

4. Who do the girls have to meet at the fountain?

_____

5. Why isn't Carmen hungry anymore?

_____

VOCABULARY

Complete each sentence. Use a word from the box.

hungry	finished	total	dozen	else

1. Twelve eggs are a _____ eggs.

2. It's three o'clock. I didn't eat lunch today. I'm so _____!

3. I need eggs, milk, and . . . what _____ do I need? Oh, I need crackers.

4. I have one more question. I'm almost _____ with this
vocabulary exercise.

5. The eggs cost two dollars. The milk costs two dollars and seventy-five cents. The
_____ is four dollars and seventy-five cents.

Grammar 1

Count and Non-Count Nouns

A. Look at the food items below. Circle the items that can be counted. Box the items that cannot be counted.

(potatoes)   [milk]   carrots   cookies   lemonade   apples

eggs   bread   beef   cheese   onions   bananas

coffee   rice   enchiladas   lettuce   crackers   broccoli

B. Look at the picture. Write the names and amounts of the food items. Use words from the box and numbers for the amounts.

| pound | gallon | cup | glass | slice | piece | dozen |

1. _____*six carrots*_____   7. _____

2. ____*two pounds of beef*____   8. _____

3. _____   9. _____

4. _____   10. _____

5. _____   11. _____

6. _____   12. _____

Name _____ Date _____

Grammar 2

Some and any

A. Look at Pablo's mother's refrigerator. Check (✔) the items you see.

1. ✔ onions
2. ☐ apples
3. ☐ lettuce
4. ☐ broccoli
5. ☐ coffee
6. ☐ carrots
7. ☐ bread
8. ☐ milk
9. ☐ lemonade
10. ☐ bananas
11. ☐ eggs
12. ☐ cheese
13. ☐ beef

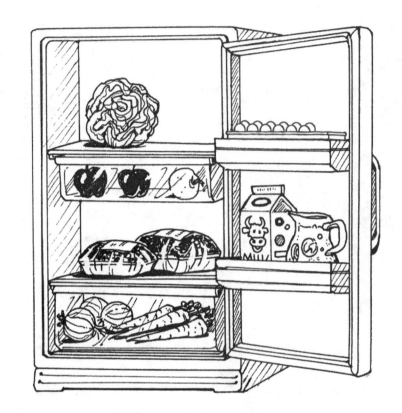

B. Look at the picture in Exercise A. Answer the questions below. Use *some* or *any*.

1. Does Pablo's mother have any onions?   *Yes, she has some onions.*

2. Does she have any cheese?   *No, she doesn't have any cheese.*

3. Does she have any broccoli?   _____

4. Does she have any milk?   _____

5. Does she have any carrots?   _____

6. Does she have any beef?   _____

C. Look in your kitchen. In your notebook, write two sentences about food items you have, and two sentences about food items you don't have. Use *some* or *any*.

Examples: *We have some lettuce.*

We don't have any bread.

Word Study

Long Vowel Sound: /ō/ as in *coat*

A. Look at the pictures and sound out the words. Fill in the blanks with *o, o___e, oa, ow,* or *oe.*

1. c___t   **2.** wind___   **3.** t___   **4.** t___st

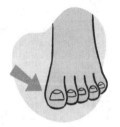

5. h___s___   **6.** c___ld   **7.** r___s___   **8.** y___-y___

B. Sound out the sentences. Circle the letters that stand for the long vowel sound /ō/. When you find one of the words, fill in a star.

1. Did you like those yellow roses?   ☆☆☆

2. There's some cold toast on the stove.   ☆☆☆

3. It's cold, so go inside and get a coat.   ☆☆☆☆

4. Oh, those pictures in your notebook are so nice!   ☆☆☆☆

C. Choose three words from Exercise A. In your notebook, write a sentence using each word.

Examples: *Do you want some toast?*

                      We don't have any pink roses.

Grammar 3

Conjunctions: *and, but,* and *so*

A. Match each phrase in the left-hand column with a phrase in the right-hand column to make sentences. Write the letter on the line.

1. _b_ I love science,   a. but I only have $20.

2. ___ I ate a lot of cookies,   b. and I love math, too.

3. ___ I have a pencil,   c. so let's make an apple pie.

4. ___ I like hamburgers,   d. so I'm not very hungry.

5. ___ That jacket costs $30,   e. but I don't have any paper.

6. ___ I have some apples,   f. and I love French fries.

B. Fill in the blanks with *and, but,* or *so.*

1. I want to buy these expensive shoes, _____*but*_____ I only have ten dollars.

2. I'm really hungry, _____ let's get something to eat.

3. I don't like coffee, _____ I love lemonade.

4. He's very nice, _____ he's cute, too.

5. We need some eggs, _____ we need some milk, too.

6. I need to get some bread, _____ let's go to the supermarket.

C. Write five sentences with *and, but,* or *so.* Use each word at least one time.

1. _We need some lettuce, but we don't need any carrots._

2. _____

3. _____

4. _____

5. _____

6. _____

Reading

A. Read "At Ricky's" on Student Book pages 130–131.
Then answer the questions.

1. Why did Mei, Maria, and Carmen go to Ricky's?

   _____

2. Who was the cashier at Ricky's?

   _____

3. Who was behind Carmen?

   _____

4. What did Carmen order?

   _____

B. Complete each sentence. Choose a word from the box. Write the word in the puzzle.

enough	ordered	receipt	customers	cashier	salad

1. We have lettuce and carrots, so let's make a _____salad_____.

2. I want to buy that coat, but I don't have _____ money.

3. There are a lot of _____ waiting in line.

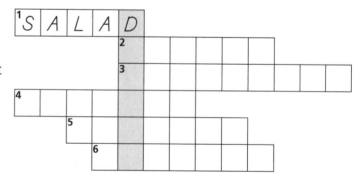

4. The _____ behind the counter said, "The total is $5.18."

5. I _____ a hamburger and French fries.

6. Amy gave the cashier $57.04. Then she asked for a _____.

C. Complete the dialogue with the new word from the puzzle.

Paco: What do you want to eat, Carmen?

Carmen: I don't know, Paco. I can't _____.

Name _____ Date _____

Writing

BEFORE YOU WRITE

A. Read the paragraph below.

I'm having a dinner party for ten friends. I want to make hamburgers and salad, so I need two pounds of beef and a dozen hamburger buns. I also need a carrot and some lettuce. For snacks, I want to get two bags of tortilla chips. I also want to have some cheese and crackers, so I need two boxes of crackers and a pound of cheese. For drinks, I need to get about six bottles of soda. And for dessert, I want to get a pie and two boxes of cookies.

B. Read the *Before I Write* checklist. Make notes on the lines below.

Before I Write

▶ Study the model.

▶ Think about food I want to serve at my dinner party.

▶ Make notes about food I want at my party.

1. What I want to make for dinner (enchiladas, hamburgers):

_____

2. What I want to have for snacks:

_____

3. What I want to have for drinks:

_____

4. What I want to have for dessert:

_____

5. What I need to buy:

_____

Writing

WRITE THIS!

Read the *While I Write* checklist. Look at your notes from Exercise B and write your paragraph.

While I Write

▶ Use words like *a*, *some*, and *four* to tell how many.
   a carrot   **some** lettuce   **two** boxes of crackers

▶ Use words like *pound*, *bag*, and *bottle* to tell how many.
   two **pounds** of beef   two **bags** of tortilla chips   six **bottles** of soda

▶ Use *and*, *but*, or *so* to connect words and ideas.
   I also want to have some cheese **and** crackers, **so** I need two boxes of crackers **and** a pound of cheese.

AFTER YOU WRITE

A. Read the *After I Write* checklist. Make corrections to your paragraph above.

After I Write

▶ Did I use words like *a*, *some*, and *four* to tell how many?

▶ Did I use words like *pound*, *bag*, and *bottle* to tell how many?

▶ Did I use *and*, *but*, or *so* to connect words and ideas?

B. Make a final copy of your paragraph in your notebook.

Chapter 12

He's the cutest guy at school.

LISTENING AND READING

Read "I Love R&B" on Student Book pages 134–135.
Then answer the questions. Use complete sentences.

1. Why does Sophie like the CD store?

   _____

2. What kind of music does Liliana like?

   _____

3. What kind of music does Paco like?

   _____

4. What CD did Sophie want to buy?

   _____

5. What did Liliana give Sophie?

   _____

VOCABULARY

Complete each sentence. Use a word from the box.

have time	section	kidding	own	age

1. My sister says she wants to give me $100, but she's just _____.

2. Kim and Lee are both fifteen. They're the same _____.

3. I never _____ to go shopping with my friends.

4. I always have to use my brother's CD player. I want my _____ CD player
   for my next birthday.

5. Beyoncé's CD is in the R&B _____ of the music store.

Grammar 1

Comparative Adjectives

A. Complete the chart with the comparative forms.

Adjective	Comparative	Adjective	Comparative	Adjective	Comparative
1. funny	_funnier_	**6.** old	_____	**11.** small	_____
2. tall	_____	**7.** young	_____	**12.** early	_____
3. short	_____	**8.** nice	_____	**13.** late	_____
4. cute	_____	**9.** silly	_____	**14.** easy	_____
5. pretty	_____	**10.** large	_____	**15.** hard	_____

B. Look at the picture. Compare the people. Use words from Exercise A.

Yoko   Ken   Lenora

1. _Ken is shorter than Yoko._

2. _____

3. _____

4. _____

C. Write sentences about members of your family. Use words from Exercise A.

1. _My sister is funnier than my brother._

2. _____

3. _____

4. _____

Grammar 2

Superlative Adjectives

A. Complete the chart with the superlative forms.

Adjective	Superlative	Adjective	Superlative	Adjective	Superlative
1. late	_latest_	6. loud	_____	11. short	_____
2. early	_____	7. silly	_____	12. cute	_____
3. small	_____	8. nice	_____	13. pretty	_____
4. large	_____	9. funny	_____	14. hard	_____
5. easy	_____	10. tall	_____	15. happy	_____

B. Complete the sentences. Use the correct form of the adjective.

1. Jim Carrey is a very ____funny____ actor.
   (funny, funnier, funniest)

2. Maria studies _____ than anyone in her English class. (hard, harder, hardest)

3. Mrs. Gomez is the _____ teacher in our school. (nice, nicer, nicest)

4. I get up _____ than my sister.
   (early, earlier, earliest)

5. Ken is the _____ person in his family.
   (short, shorter, shortest)

6. That music is so _____! (loud, louder, loudest)

7. My father is _____ than my mother. (tall, taller, tallest)

Word Study

Long Vowel Sound: /yo͞o/ as in *use*

A. Look at the pictures and sound out the words. Fill in the blanks with *u___e*, *u*, or *ew*.

1. m___l___   2. c___b___   3. f_____   4. m___n___

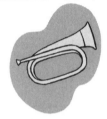

5. h___g___   6. b___gle   7. m___seum   8. n_____

B. Sound out the sentences. Circle the words with the long vowel sound /yo͞o/.

1. What a cute mule.

2. Pam is wearing her new uniform.

3. Andrew blew the bugle at the party.

4. Here are a few menus.

C. Choose five words from Exercise A. In your notebook, write a sentence for each word.

Example: *I ate a few carrots for a snack.*

Name _____ Date _____

Grammar 3

Comparatives and Superlatives with *more* and *most*

A. Write the comparative and superlative forms.

Adjective	Comparative	Superlative
1. interesting	*more interesting*	*most interesting*
2. hard	*harder*	*hardest*
3. difficult		
4. formal		
5. big		
6. casual		
7. expensive		
8. old		

B. Look at the jackets. Complete the sentences. Use the comparative or superlative.

1. The black jacket is ____*more expensive*____ than the white jacket. (expensive)

2. The gray jacket is the _____ jacket. (old)

3. The white jacket is _____ than the black jacket. (casual)

4. The black jacket is _____ than the gray jacket. (formal)

5. The black jacket is the _____ jacket. (expensive)

Reading

A. Read "Pablo's Surprise" on Student Book pages 140–141. Then answer the questions. Circle the letter of the correct answer.

1. How did the first performer look?

  a. She looked pretty.   **b.** She looked nervous.

2. Who did Maria say was funnier?

  a. Pablo   **b.** Sally

3. What did Pablo do?

  a. He told a funny story.   **b.** He played the guitar, sang, and read a poem.

4. What was Pablo's big secret?

  a. He was a performer in a show.   **b.** He was writing poetry.

5. Who was the author of the poem?

  a. Pablo Sanchez   **b.** Jorge Luján

B. Complete each sentence. Use a word from the box. Write the words in the puzzle.

| stage | performer | author | audience | storyteller | section |

1. The _storyteller_ told a wonderful story.

2. Everyone in the _____ loved Pablo's song.

3. The music store in my town has the best reggae music _____.

4. The children clapped when the singer walked on the _____.

5. Justin Timberlake is my favorite _____. His shows are great!

6. J.K. Rowling is a great _____. She writes the Harry Potter books.

Pablo was the best _____ in the show!

Writing

BEFORE YOU WRITE

A. Read the paragraph below.

> There are four people in my family: my brother, my father, my grandmother, and me. I'm the youngest person. I'm twelve years old and I'm very tall. My brother is fourteen. He's shorter than me, but he's older than me. Actually, my brother is the shortest person in the family. My father is funny. He likes to tell jokes. Sometimes he's very silly. My grandmother is the most talented person in the family. She paints, plays the piano, and is the best cook!

B. Read the *Before I Write* checklist. Make notes on the lines below.

Before I Write
▶ Study the model.
▶ Think about my family.
▶ Make notes about my family.

1. Who the people in my family are:

   _____

2. How old and how tall they are:

   _____

3. What's special about each person:

   _____

Writing

WRITE THIS!

Read the *While I Write* checklist. Look at your notes from Exercise B and write your paragraph.

While I Write

▶ Use comparative adjectives with *-er* or *more* to compare two people or things.
  *My brother is **older** than me.*

▶ Use superlative adjectives with *-est* or *most* to compare two or more people or things.
  *I'm the **youngest** person.*
  *My grandmother is the **most talented** person in the family.*

▶ Give more information about each person.
  *He likes to tell jokes. Sometimes he's **very** silly.*

AFTER YOU WRITE

A. Check your paragraph. Read the *After I Write* checklist. Make corrections to your paragraph above.

After I Write

▶ Did I use comparative adjectives with *-er* or *more* to compare two people or things?

▶ Did I use superlative adjectives with *-est* or *most* to compare two or more people or things?

▶ Did I give more information about each person?

B. Make a final copy of your paragraph in your notebook.

Chapter 13

He's going to fall!

LISTENING AND READING

Read "The Accident" on Student Book pages 146–147. Write *True* or *False* for each statement.

1. Carlos says he can skate on one foot. _____

2. Carmen and Liliana say Carlos is going to fall. _____

3. Liliana is going to ask Carlos to give her some skating lessons. _____

4. Carlos hurt his head. _____

5. Liliana is going to call 911. _____

VOCABULARY

Complete the dialogue. Use words from the box.

hurts	fell	fast	broke	emergency

Ring . . . ring . . . ring

911: Hello. 911.

Carmen: Hello? Hello! We have an (**1**) _____! My brother was skating

very (**2**) _____. He (**3**) _____ down. I think he

(**4**) _____ his arm!

911: It sounds like an emergency!

Carmen: It is! *Please* hurry. His arm really (**5**) _____!

Grammar 1

Future Tense with *be going to*: Statements

A. Write sentences using the future tense with *be going to*. Use contractions.

1. I / stay home / on Saturday (negative) *I'm not going to stay home on Saturday.*

2. My sister / baby-sit / tomorrow (affirmative) _____

3. My family / go out for dinner / tonight (negative) _____

4. We / eat Chinese food / on Sunday (affirmative) _____

B. Write sentences about what you and your family are going to do on Saturday.

1. *My sister is going to go to her dance lesson.*

2. _____

3. _____

4. _____

Future Tense with *be going to*: Yes / No Questions

Fill in the blanks with the correct form of *be going to*. Then complete the answers. Use contractions in negative answers.

1. ___*Are*___ you _____*going to*_____ study English tonight?

   No, *I'm not.* _____

2. _____ your brother _____ play basketball this weekend?

   No, _____

3. _____ you and your friends _____ go to a movie on Friday?

   No, _____

4. _____ your parents _____ clean the house on Saturday?

   Yes, _____

5. _____ your best friend _____ call you tonight?

   No, _____

Grammar 2

Future Tense with *be going to*: Information Questions

A. Read the questions. Then write true answers about tomorrow.

1. When are you going to get up?

   I'm going to get up at seven.

2. What are you going to do first?

   _____

3. What are you going to eat for breakfast?

   _____

4. Who is going to make your breakfast?

   _____

5. Where are you going to go after breakfast?

   _____

B. Make information questions. Match the beginning of the question in the left-hand column with the correct ending in the right-hand column. Write the letters.

1. _*b*_ What are we   **a.** going to go after school?

2. ____ Who are they   **b.** going to do at the party?

3. ____ What is he   **c.** going to see the movie with?

4. ____ When is she   **d.** going to ask his grandmother for?

5. ____ Where are you   **e.** going to do her homework?

C. Answer the questions.

1. What are you going to do this weekend?

   _____

2. Who are you going to be with?

   _____

Word Study

Other Vowel Sound: /o͞o/ as in *school*

A. Look at the pictures and sound out the words. Fill in the blanks with *u___e*, *ue*, *ew*, or *oo*.

1. gl _____   **2.** fl _____   **3.** m _____ n   **4.** J ___ n ___

5. dr _____   **6.** sch _____ l   **7.** fl ___ t ___   **8.** sp _____ n

B. Read the poem. Circle the words with the vowel sound /o͞o/.

'Twas in the month of June

I heard a merry tune—

A bird's song like a flute

Beneath the bright blue moon.

C. Choose two words from Exercise A. In your notebook, write a sentence using each word.

Example: *Last night I saw the moon from*
           my window.

Grammar 3

Commands

A. Complete the sentences. Write the letters.

1. _c_ We're late,
2. ___ I can't hear the teacher,
3. ___ It's loud in the hallway,
4. ___ I think you broke your leg,
5. ___ It's hot in here,
6. ___ We're going to have a test now,
7. ___ The stove is hot,

a. so please close the door.
b. so please open the window.
c. so please hurry!
d. so be careful!
e. so please close your books.
f. so please be quiet.
g. so don't stand up!

B. Look at the picture. What does the teacher say? Write commands from the box.

> Close the window!   Please be quiet.   Close your book.
> Please sit down.   Don't look up!

1. _Please sit down._   4. _____

2. _____   5. _____

3. _____

Reading

A. Read "The Visitors" on Student Book pages 152–153. Fill in the blanks. Choose phrases from the box.

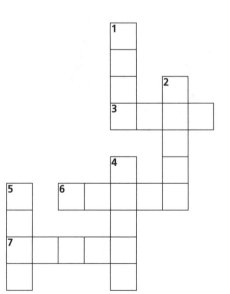

brought his guitar	gave him a CD	sprained his ankle
hurt a lot	came to visit him	watched TV
went to the hospital	brought some cookies	

Carlos broke his wrist and (**1**) _____

On Saturday, he (**2**) _____.

On Sunday and Monday, Carlos (**3**) _____.

On Tuesday, his friends (**4**) _____.

Maria and Liliana (**5**) _____. Samir and Bic

(**6**) _____. Pablo (**7**) _____.

Carlos said his wrist and ankle (**8**) _____, so Carmen said, "We'll

come back later." Then Carlos shouted, "I feel great! Don't go!"

B. Complete the puzzle. Read each clue and choose the correct word from the box.

bored	awake	leap	pain	shout	visit	weak

ACROSS

3. what you feel when something hurts

6. talk really loud

7. not sleeping

DOWN

1. jump high in the air

2. spend time with someone

4. tired because you have nothing to do

5. not strong

Writing

BEFORE YOU WRITE

A. Read the paragraph below.

> *Next week is going to be fun. I'm going to visit my aunt and uncle. Every morning I'm going to baby-sit my cousin. I'm going to play games and read books with him. We're going to go to the park, too. Every afternoon, I'm going to go to the swimming pool or to the movies with my older cousins. On Saturday, the whole family is going to go to the beach. It's going to be a great week!*

B. Read the *Before I Write* checklist. Make notes on the lines below.

Before I Write

▶ Study the model.

▶ Think about what I'm going to do this summer.

▶ Make notes about what I'm going to do this summer.

1. What I'm going to do:

_____

_____

2. Who I'm going to be with:

_____

_____

3. Where and when I'm going to go:

_____

_____

Writing

WRITE THIS!

Read the *While I Write* checklist. Look at your notes from page 113 and write your paragraph.

While I Write

▶ Use *be going to* to tell about the future.
   *Next week **is going to** be fun.*

▶ Use phrases to tell when something is going to happen.
   ***Every afternoon,** I'm going to go to the swimming pool.*
   ***On Saturday**, the whole family is going to go to the beach.*

▶ Use contractions for subject pronouns + *be* in informal writing.
   ***It's** going to be a great week!*

AFTER YOU WRITE

A. Read the *After I Write* checklist. Make corrections to your paragraph above.

After I Write

▶ Did I use *be going to* to tell about the future?

▶ Did I use phrases to tell when something is going to happen?

▶ Did I use contractions for subject pronouns + *be*?

B. Make a final copy of your paragraph in your notebook.

Chapter 14

Hey! The lights went out!

A. Read "The Storm" on Student Book pages 156–157.
Then answer the questions. Write complete sentences.

1. What did Carlos see outside?

   _____

2. Why did the school's electricity go off?

   _____

3. What was Pablo doing when the lights went out?

   _____

B. Read these sentences about "The Storm." Put the sentences in order.
Number them from 1 to 5.

____ The lights went out.

____ The buses came.

_/_ Mrs. Kim was talking about weather.

____ Mrs. Kim asked Carlos to sit down.

____ The principal said they were closing the school.

VOCABULARY

Complete each sentence. Use a word from the box.

continue	soon	storm

1. Don't stop working now. Please _____ your lesson.

2. The movie will start _____. It's going to start in about two minutes.

3. The sky is gray. It sure is getting dark outside. A _____ is coming.

Grammar 1

Past Continuous Tense: Statements

A. Write an affirmative and a negative sentence for each picture. Use the past continuous. Use contractions.

1. talk / eat lunch   *They were talking. They weren't eating lunch.*

2. play a game / study   _____

                              _____

3. listen to music / read _____

                              _____

B. In your notebook, write four sentences using the past continuous. Use four of the phrases from the box.

| yesterday afternoon | last night | this morning | last Saturday | Sunday evening |

Example: *I was baby-sitting last Saturday.*

Past Continuous Tense: *Yes / No* Questions

Fill in the blanks with *Was* or *Were*. Then write true short answers. Use contractions.

1. __*Were*__ you sleeping yesterday morning at seven? *No, I wasn't.* _____

2. _____ your friends eating lunch yesterday at noon? _____

3. _____ your English teacher in school yesterday? _____

4. _____ your friend watching TV last night? _____

5. _____ it raining this morning? _____

Grammar 2

Past Continuous Tense: Information Questions

A. Match the questions and answers. Write the letters.

1. ___ What was Jon doing last night?   a. They were sitting at the kitchen table.

2. ___ Who was helping him?   b. He was studying for a math test.

3. ___ When was he studying?   c. They were eating popcorn.

4. ___ Where were they sitting?   d. He was studying at seven.

5. ___ What else were they doing?   e. His mother was helping him.

B. Look at David's schedule for last Saturday. Write information questions. Use the past continuous.

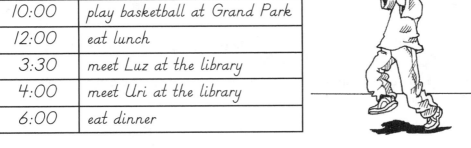

Saturday	
10:00	play basketball at Grand Park
12:00	eat lunch
3:30	meet Luz at the library
4:00	meet Uri at the library
6:00	eat dinner

1. **Q:** (What) _What was David doing at ten?_____

   A: He was playing basketball at ten.

2. **Q:** (Where) _____

   A: He was playing basketball at Grand Park.

3. **Q:** (When) _____

   A: He was eating lunch at noon.

4. **Q:** (Who) _____.

   A: He was meeting Luz at the library.

5. **Q:** (Who else) _____.

   A: He was also meeting Uri at the library.

6. **Q:** (When) _____

   A: He was eating dinner at six.

Word Study

Other Vowel Sound: /o͝o/ as in *look*

A. Look at the pictures and sound out the words. Fill in the blanks with *oo*.

  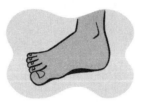 

1. c_____kie   **2.** g_____d-bye   **3.** f_____t   **4.** noteb_____k

5. c_____k   **6.** h_____k   **7.** b_____k   **8.** h_____d

B. Sound out the words in each column. Check "yes" if all the words have the vowel sound /o͝o/. Check "no" if they do not.

1. football	2. look	3. shampoo	4. book
cook	moon	cookies	good-bye
food	foot	took	notebook
☐ yes ☐ no	☐ yes ☐ no	☐ yes ☐ no	☐ yes ☐ no

C. Choose three words from Exercise A. In your notebook, write a sentence using each word.

Example: *I don't like to say good-bye.*

Grammar 3

Possessive Pronouns

Complete the sentences. Use possessive pronouns.

1. That's my CD.   It's ____*mine*____.

4. That's her CD.   It's _____.

2. That's your CD. It's _____.

5. That's their CD.   It's _____.

3. That's his CD.   It's _____.

6. That's our CD.   It's _____.

Questions with *whose*

Look at the pictures. Write the question or the answer. Use possesive pronouns.

1. Whose guitar is that?

It's his. _____

2. Whose umbrellas are those?

_____

3. Whose cats are those?

_____

4. _____ (notebook)

It's hers.

5. _____ (videos)

They're his.

6. Whose bike is that?

_____

Name _____ Date _____

Reading

A. Read "Mother's Plan" on Student Book pages 162–163. Write *True* or *False* for each statement.

1. Washington School was closed for two days. _____

2. There was a thunderstorm on the second day the students stayed home. _____

3. Mrs. Alvarez wanted Carlos and Carmen to watch TV. _____

4. Carlos's broken leg was hurting. _____

5. Carlos didn't clean his room. _____

6. Carmen's mother asked her to do Carlos's homework. _____

7. Carmen talked on the phone after supper. _____

8. Carmen enjoyed the beautiful weather on Saturday. _____

B. Complete each sentence. Use a word from the box. Write one letter on each line. Then write the circled letters to answer the question.

closed	completely	ending	instead	perfect	raining	sunny	weather

1. The show is (e) n d i n g . It will finish in five minutes.

2. It's not raining at all now. The rain has stopped __ __ __ __ Ⓞ __ Ⓞ __ .

3. It's just right. It's __ __ __ __ __ ⓄⓄ!

4. How's the __ __ __ __ __ Ⓞ today? Is it sunny, rainy, cloudy, or snowy?

5. Get your umbrella. It's __ __ Ⓞ __ __ __ __ outside.

6. That store is not open today. It's Ⓞ __ __ __ __ __ .

7. She isn't doing her homework. She's talking on the phone Ⓞ __ __ Ⓞ __ __ __ .

8. It's a beautiful day today. It's __ __ __ __ Ⓞ and warm.

What didn't Washington School have for two days?

__ __ __ __ __ __ __ __ __ __ __ __ __

Name _____ Date _____

Writing

A. Read the paragraph below.

> Last Saturday was my sister's eighth birthday. My family had a party for her. Around 12:00 we started getting ready. My father was making hamburgers and my mother was cleaning the table. I was inside with my sister. Suddenly there was a loud noise. My father looked up. A plane was writing "Happy 8th . . ." in the sky. My father yelled, "Look outside, Kim! Look up!" My sister and I ran to the window. The plane was finishing a sentence. The sentence read "Happy 8th Birthday, Kim!"

B. Read the *Before I Write* checklist. Make notes on the lines below.

Before I Write

▶ Study the model.

▶ Think of a funny, exciting, or dangerous event that happened to me.

▶ Make notes about an event that happened to me.

1. Where I was and what I was doing before the event happened:

_____

_____

2. What the event was:

_____

_____

3. What happened during and after the event:

_____

_____

Writing

WRITE THIS!

Read the *While I Write* checklist. Look at your notes from page 121 and write your paragraph.

While I Write

▶ Use the past continuous tense to tell what people were doing when the event happened.

*My father was **making** hamburgers and my mother was **cleaning** the table.*

▶ Use the simple past tense to tell about the event and what happened next.

*Suddenly there **was** a loud noise.*
*My father **looked** up.*

▶ Use quotation marks around the exact words that a person says.

My dad yelled, "Look outside, Kim! Look up!"

AFTER YOU WRITE

A. Read the *After I Write* checklist. Make corrections to your paragraph above.

After I Write

▶ Did I use the past continuous tense to tell what people were doing when the event happened?

▶ Did I use the simple past tense to tell about the event and what happened next?

▶ Did I use quotation marks around the exact words that a person said?

B. Make a final copy of your paragraph in your notebook.

Name _____ Date _____

Chapter 15

We'll have a study group.

LISTENING AND READING

Read "Help for Maria" on Student Book pages 166–167.
What will the students do to get ready for the test?
Complete the sentences.

1. They'll start a _____*study group*_____.

2. They'll ask their parents to come to a _____.

3. They'll study the _____ words.

4. They'll review the _____ in their book.

5. They'll _____ one story every day.

VOCABULARY

Complete each sentence. Use a word from the box.

exam	extra	final	meeting	group	review

1. I wasn't at school yesterday, so I have _____ homework tonight.

2. We have a big math test next week. It's the final _____.

3. I need to _____ the vocabulary words for the test on Friday.

4. Today is the last day to buy school T-shirts. It's the _____ day
   of the T-shirt sale.

5. We need to decide what to do for our science project. We need to talk to
   the _____.

6. We're having a _____ tonight. Come to the cafeteria at seven.

Grammar 1

Future Tense with *will*: Statements

A. Complete the sentences with *will* and a phrase from the box.
Use contractions.

buy some soda   study a lot   finish their homework
clean my room   go to bed early

1. He's nervous about the final exam, so_____ *he'll study a lot* _____ this week.

2. We're having a birthday party tomorrow, so_____ today.

3. My friend is coming over later, so_____ now.

4. She's sleepy, so_____ tonight.

5. They're going to the movies tonight, so_____ in
   the afternoon.

B. Change each sentence from the affirmative to the negative. Use *won't*.

1. I'll go to bed early tonight. ⟶ ___ *I won't* ___ go to bed early tonight.

2. It will rain tomorrow. ⟶ _____ rain tomorrow.

3. I'll call a friend tonight. ⟶ _____ call a friend tonight.

4. They'll start a study group. ⟶ _____ start a study group.

Future Tense with *will*: Yes/No Questions

Change the sentences in Exercise B to yes/no questions. Then write true short answers.

1. **A:** *Will you go to bed early tonight?* _____
   B: *No, I won't.* _____

2. **A:** _____
   B: _____

3. **A:** _____
   B: _____

4. **A:** _____
   B: _____

Grammar 2

Future Tense with *will*: Information Questions

A. Read the answers. Write information questions. Use *who*, *what*, *when*, or *where*.

1. *Who will make plans for the study group?*   Everyone will make plans for the study group.

2. _____   They'll meet at the library.

3. _____   They'll study vocabulary words.

4. _____   They'll meet every Wednesday afternoon.

5. _____   They'll bring their books.

6. _____   They'll bring their notebooks, too.

B. Write questions to complete the dialogue. Use *Who*, *What*, *When*, or *Where* and future tense with *will*.

1. **A:** *When will you visit Guatemala again?*

   B: I'll visit Guatemala again this summer.

2. **A:** _____?

   B: My sister and brother will go with me.

3. **A:** _____?

   B: We'll stay at our cousin's apartment.

4. **A:** _____?

   B: We'll visit our friends and family.

5. **A:** _____?

   B: We'll see the new museum.

6. **A:** _____?

   B: We'll also see an outdoor art show.

Word Study

Other Vowel Sound: /ô/ as in *saw*

A. Look at the pictures and sound out the words. Fill in the blanks with *au* or *aw*.

1. _____thor

2. p_____

3. dr_____

4. _____gust

5. str_____

6. y_____n

7. l_____ndry

8. str_____berry

B. Sound out the sentences. Circle the words with the vowel sound /ô/. When you find one of the words, fill in a star.

1. The audience was yawning. ★★☆

2. The author was doing his laundry. ☆☆☆

3. I saw Paul last autumn. ☆☆☆

4. In August we drink strawberry sodas with a straw. ☆☆☆

C. Choose three words from Exercise A. In your notebook, write a sentence using each word.

Example: *The trees look pretty in August.*

Grammar 3

Statements with *may* and *might*

A. Write these words in the correct boxes: *going to, not going to, may, may not, might, might not, will, won't.*

Definite plans	Possible plans
going to	_____
_____	_____
_____	_____
_____	_____

B. Rewrite the sentences. Change the definite plans to possible plans.

1. We're not going to go shopping.

   (may) _____*We may not go shopping.*_____

2. I'm going to go out with my friends.

   (may) _____

3. He'll be late.

   (might) _____

4. They won't have a party.

   (might) _____

5. She's not going to buy a dress.

   (may) _____

6. They're going to have a study group on Thursday.

   (might) _____

C. Write three sentences about your possible plans for tomorrow.
Use *may, may not, might,* and *might not.*

1. _*I might wear a blue sweater and jeans.*_

2. _____

3. _____

4. _____

Reading

A. Read "Grandmother Chu" on Student Book pages 172–173. Then answer the questions. Write complete sentences.

1. Who does Mei live with?

_____

2. What language does Mei's grandmother speak?

_____

3. Why didn't Mei's grandmother want to go to the meeting at the school?

_____

4. What did Mei's grandmother always want to do?

_____

5. Who taught Mei's grandmother to read Chinese?

_____

B. Complete each sentence. Use words from the box.

| softly | nodded | whispered | translator | lit up |

1. Her grandmother _____ her head up and down to say, "Yes."

2. Their eyes _____ when they talked about their family in China.

3. She spoke very _____ in English class because she was very nervous.

4. The _____ helped the new students learn the new vocabulary.

5. I quietly _____ to my friend at the study group, "Thank you for your help!"

Writing

BEFORE YOU WRITE

A. Read the paragraph below.

> *I lived in Guilin, China, for thirteen years. This summer, I'll go back with my mom and dad to visit. Guilin is a small city, but it is very beautiful. The people are nice, and the food is very, very good. We'll stay at my grandmother's house and eat good Chinese food. We'll visit my aunt and uncle. I might meet some new cousins. I'll go out with my old friends, too. We'll go shopping. We may see the newest Chinese movie. And, of course, we'll catch up on all the family news!*

B. Read the *Before I Write* checklist. Make notes on the lines below.

Before I Write

▶ Study the model.

▶ Think about a trip I plan to take someday.

▶ Make notes about my trip.

1. Where I'll go and who I'll go with:

_____

_____

2. What the place is like:

_____

_____

3. Where I'll stay, who I'll see, and what I'll do:

_____

_____

Writing

WRITE THIS!

Read the *While I Write* checklist. Look at your notes from page 129 and write your paragraph.

While I Write

▶ Use *will* or the contraction *'ll* to talk about your future plans.
   We'll stay at my grandmother's house.

▶ Use *may* and *might* to talk about possible future plans.
   I might meet some new cousins.
   We may see the newest Chinese movie.

▶ Use the present tense to describe a place.
   Guilin is a small city, but it is very beautiful.

AFTER YOU WRITE

A. Read the *After I Write* checklist. Make corrections to your paragraph above.

After I Write

▶ Did I use *will* or its contraction *'ll* to talk about my future plans?

▶ Did I use *may* and *might* to talk about possible future plans?

▶ Did I use the present tense to describe the place?

B. Make a final copy of your paragraph in your notebook.

Chapter 16

I sometimes study with my friends.

LISTENING AND READING

Read "The Study Group" on Student Book pages 178–179. Then answer the questions. Write complete sentences.

1. What does Carlos like doing at the study group?

_____

2. What does Maria want to start doing?

_____

3. How often does Carmen study English?

_____

4. How often does Maria have to study English?

_____

5. What does Sophie have every afternoon?

_____

VOCABULARY

Complete each sentence. Use a word from the box.

especially	mind	practice	chance	typical

1. Do you _____ if I have another sandwich? I'm still hungry.

2. We go to soccer _____ three times a week.

3. I like ice cream, _____ chocolate ice cream. It's my favorite!

4. Tonight is the last night of the show. Don't miss the _____ to see it.

5. Enchiladas and empanadas are _____ Mexican foods.

Grammar 1

Adverbs of Frequency

A. Write the adverbs of frequency in the graph. Use words from the box.

| often   sometimes   never   usually   always |

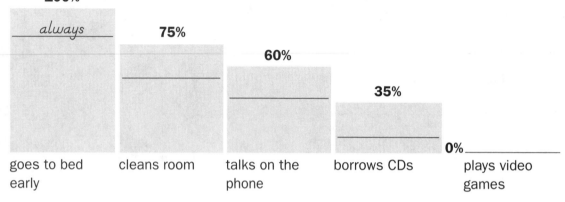

Marco's Sunday Schedule

100%
always
75%
60%
35%
0%

goes to bed early   cleans room   talks on the phone   borrows CDs   plays video games

B. Look at the graph in exercise A. Complete the sentences with the adverbs of frequency.

1. Marco ___*usually*___ cleans his room.

2. He _____ goes to bed early.

3. He _____ borrows CDs.

4. He _____ talks on the phone.

5. He _____ plays video games.

C. Look at the activities in Exercise A. In your notebook, write two true statements about yourself. Use adverbs of frequency.

Adverbs of Frequency with *be*

Write sentences using adverbs of frequency and *be*. Use contractions.

1. she / always / on time for school   ___*She's always on time for school.*___

2. they / never / late for the movies   _____

3. he / often / bored on weekends   _____

4. I / sometimes / nervous before a test   _____

5. she / usually / shy at parties   _____

6. we / always / happy to baby-sit   _____

Name _____ Date _____

Grammar 2

How often and Expressions of Frequency

A. Read the questions and write true answers. Use expressions of frequency or the adverb *never*.

Expressions of Frequency	
one time / once	a day
two times / twice	a week
three times	a month
four times	a year

1. How often do you go to the movies?

   I go to the movies twice a month.

2. How often are you late to class?

   _____

3. How often does your English class meet?

   _____

4. How often do you go swimming?

   _____

5. How often do you talk on the phone?

   _____

B. Write three *how often* questions. Use ideas from the box or your own ideas.

dry the dishes	go shopping	listen to music
play soccer	read a book	study with a friend
visit your grandparents	watch TV	

Example: You: *How often do you read a book?*

1. You: _____

2. You: _____

3. You: _____

C. Interview a friend or family member. Ask the questions in Exercise B. In your notebooks, write their answers using expressions of frequency.

Example: Friend / Family Member: *I read a book once a day.*

Word Study

Other vowel sound: /oi/ as in *enjoy*

A. Look at the pictures and sound out the words. Fill in the blanks with *oi* or *oy*.

1. s_____l **2.** c_____n **3.** b_____ **4.** p_____nt

5. t_____ **6.** b_____l **7.** R_____ **8.** f_____l

B. Sound out the sentences. Circle the words with the vowel sound / oi /.
When you find one of the words, fill in a star.

1. He saw a (coin) in the (soil)   ★★☆☆

2. Don't put oil in the soil!   ☆☆☆☆

3. We need to buy oil, potatoes, and foil.   ☆☆☆☆

4. Roy enjoys seeing coins from other countries.   ☆☆☆☆

5. The little boy is pointing to his toy.   ☆☆☆☆

6. She watched the oil boil in the pot.   ☆☆☆☆

C. Choose two words from Exercise A. In your notebook, write a sentence
using each word.

Example: *Look at that old coin!*

Grammar 3

Gerunds as Objects of Verbs

A. Write five true sentences about yourself, your family, and your friends. Choose verbs and verb phrases from the boxes.

love	play sports	do homework
enjoy	clean the house	listen to music
like	talk on the phone	go to parties
not like	study science	watch videos
hate	go swimming	dance
	wash dishes	cook
	go out to eat	stay up late
	get up early	stay home from school

Example: *My father loves going out to eat.*

1. _____

2. _____

3. _____

4. _____

5. _____

B. Write five *yes/no* questions using *like* and *enjoy* and the phrases in Exercise A. Then write true short answers.

Example: **A:** *Do you like studying science?* **B:** *No, I don't.*

  A: *Does your best friend enjoy listening to music?* **B:** *Yes, she does.*

1. **A:** _____ **B:** _____

2. **A:** _____ **B:** _____

3. **A:** _____ **B:** _____

4. **A:** _____ **B:** _____

5. **A:** _____ **B:** _____

Name _____ **Date** _____

Reading

A. Read "The Dancer" on Student Book pages 184–185. Then answer each question.
Circle the letter of the correct answer.

1. What is Sophie's favorite free-time activity?

   a. dancing

   b. studying with friends

2. What is one of Sophie's favorite memories?

   a. being a student at Washington school

   b. dancing in a festival

3. What does Sophie think about dancing?

   a. it's easier than it looks

   b. it's fun and it's great exercise

4. How often does the study group meet?

   a. three times a month

   b. three times a week

5. Why does Sophie like being with other people when she studies?

   a. so she doesn't get bored

   b. so she can have snacks

B. Complete the puzzle. Read each definition and choose the correct word from the box.

dancer	dancing	exercise	friendly	snack
including	intelligent	join	myself	celebration

ACROSS

4. a small amount of food eaten between meals

6. physical activity

8. a person who dances

10. moving to music

DOWN

1. very smart

2. another name for *me*

3. nice and easy to be with

5. a party you have when something good happens

7. bringing into a group

9. begin to take part in an activity

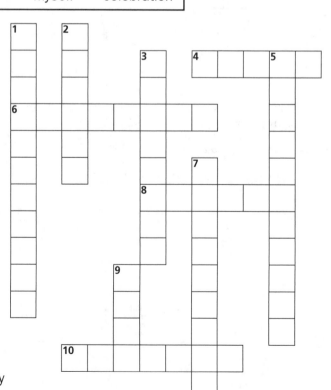

Writing

BEFORE YOU WRITE

A. Read the paragraph below.

> I love listening to music. I usually listen to music two or three times a day. I always listen to music in the morning when I am getting ready for school, and I often listen to music after school when I am reading or doing my homework. I started listening to music a lot when I was twelve. In Mexico I usually listened to Spanish music, but now I listen to Spanish and English music. My favorite singer is Enrique Iglesias. I have all his CDs!

B. Read the *Before I Write* checklist. Make notes on the lines below.

Before I Write

▶ Study the model.

▶ Think about my favorite free-time activity.

▶ Make notes about my favorite free-time activity.

1. How often and when I do my favorite free-time activity:

_____

2. When I first became interested in my favorite free-time activity:

_____

_____

3. Details about my favorite free-time activity:

_____

_____

Writing

WRITE THIS!

Read the *While I Write* checklist. Look at your notes from page 137 and write your paragraph.

While I Write

▶ Use gerunds to tell about what I like to do.

I love **listening** *to music.*

▶ Use adverbs of frequency (*always, usually, often, sometimes,* and *never*)
to tell how often I do something.

I **often** *listen to music after school.*

▶ Use words and phrases that tell how often I do something.

I usually listen to music **two or three times a day**.

AFTER YOU WRITE

A. Read the *After I Write* checklist. Make corrections to your paragraph above.

After I Write

▶ Did I use gerunds to tell about what I like to do?

▶ Did I use adverbs of frequency to tell how often I do something?

▶ Did I use words and phrases that tell how often I do something?

B. Make a final copy of your paragraph in your notebook.

Chapter 17

You should get some rest.

Read "At the Nurse's Office" on Student Book pages 188–189.
Rewrite the sentences to make them true.

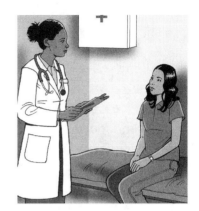

1. Maria tells Mr. Gomez she feels <u>okay</u>.

   Maria tells Mr. Gomez she feels terrible.

2. Mr. Gomez tells Maria to go see <u>the school principal</u>.

   _____

3. Mr. Gomez tells Carmen <u>to go home</u>.

   _____

4. Maria has <u>a sore arm, a stomachache, and a bad headache</u>.

   _____

5. Ms. Cho says English <u>isn't hard</u>.

   _____

6. Ms. Cho tells Maria she should <u>get some medicine</u>.

   _____

7. Ms. Cho tells Maria to call a doctor <u>in a couple of days</u>.

   _____

8. Ms. Cho tells Maria she should <u>go back to Mr. Gomez's class</u>.

   _____

VOCABULARY

Look at the pictures. Match each word with a picture. Write the letter.

1. _____ stomachache

2. _____ headache

3. _____ sore throat

a.

b.

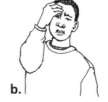
c.

Grammar 1

Statements with *should*

Write sentences about what to do when you are sick.
Use *should* and *shouldn't*.

1. (drink water and juice)

   You should drink a lot of water and juice.

2. (see a doctor)

   _____

3. (go to school)

   _____

4. (get plenty of rest)

   _____

5. (play soccer)

   _____

Yes/No Questions with *should*

A. Write three *yes/no* questions asking a friend for advice. Use *should*.

1. *Should I buy this CD?* _____

2. _____

3. _____

4. _____

B. Write three *yes/no* questions asking a friend to agree with you. Use *shouldn't*.

1. *Shouldn't we invite Natasha to the party?*

2. _____

3. _____

4. _____

Grammar 2

Statements with *could*

A. Complete the dialogues. Write sentences with *could*. Use phrases from the box.

baby-sit	go to the cafeteria	get a book at the library
get some rest	start a study group	ride your bike to school

1. **A:** I'm hungry. **B:** *You could go to the cafeteria.* _____

2. **A:** I need to earn some money. **B:** _____

3. **A:** I want to read something. **B:** _____

4. **A:** I should get more exercise. **B:** _____

5. **A:** I want to do better in school. **B:** _____

6. **A:** I'm very tired. **B:** _____

B. Match the problems with the suggestions. Write the letters.

____ 1. I need to buy some jeans.   **a.** You could go to the new department store.

____ 2. I want to help my mom.   **b.** You could study with me tonight.

____ 3. I have to get an A on the math test!   **c.** You could see the new Johnny Depp movie.

____ 4. I don't know what movie to see.   **d.** You could wash and dry the dishes.

____ 5. What can I get for Ben's birthday?   **e.** You could get him a CD.

Word Study

Other vowel sound: /ou/ as in *out*

A. Look at the pictures and sound out the words. Fill in the blanks with *ou* or *ow*.

1. m_____se   **2.** cr_____d   **3.** h_____se   **4.** cl_____d

5. t_____n   **6.** eyebr_____   **7.** _____l   **8.** m_____th

B. Fill in the blanks. Use *ou* or *ow*.

1. Mom f_____nd a m_____se under the c_____ch.

2. There was a cr_____d at Gino's h_____se on Saturday.

3. The o_____ stayed in the tree all night.

C. Choose four words from Exercise A. In your notebook,
write a sentence using each word.

Example: *He lives in this town.*

Grammar 3

Because Clauses

A. Match the statements with the *because* clauses. Write the letters.

_f_ **1.** I like playing basketball

____ **2.** I love video games

____ **3.** I enjoy baby-sitting

____ **4.** I hate cleaning my room

____ **5.** I enjoy going to parties

____ **6.** I don't like crowds

a. because they're exciting.

b. because I like children.

c. because they make me feel nervous.

d. because I like meeting people.

e. because it's a lot of work.

f. because it's good exercise.

B. Complete the sentences. Use *because* and the clauses in the box.

he's always hungry	he was at soccer practice
it's boring to study alone	she had a dance class
she feels terrible	she has a test tomorrow

1. Pablo likes having a study group _because it's_
boring to study alone .

2. Carlos was late for the study group _____
_____ .

3. Maria should go to the school nurse _____
_____ .

4. Maria is worried _____ .

5. Sophie was late _____ .

6. Carlos likes snacks _____ .

Name _____ Date _____

Reading

A. Read "The Artist" on Student Book pages 194–195.
Then answer the questions. Write complete sentences.

1. Why were Maria's friends worried about her?

_____

2. Why do Maria's friends think she'll do well on the test?

_____

3. What do Maria's friends learn about her?

_____

4. How does Maria feel after talking with her friends?

_____

B. Complete each sentence. Choose a word from the box. Write the word in the puzzle. Then complete the sentence with the new word from the puzzle.

stay	knock	smart	surprised	flowers	idea

1. The girls were _____ to see their new teacher at the restaurant.

2. Carlos gave Maria some _____ to make her feel better.

3. I have no _____ what time it is because I lost my watch.

4. Marco said, "There's a _____ at the door. Maybe the pizza is here!"

5. My bird can say "Hello." It's very _____.

6. Students who are sick have to _____ home from school.

There was _____ of food at the surprise party.

Writing

BEFORE YOU WRITE

A. Read the paragraph below.

> What should you do when you visit my city, New York City? First, you should visit the Empire State Building, because it's the tallest building in New York. You can walk around the top of the building and see the whole city. Next, you could visit an art museum, the zoo in Central Park, or the Statue of Liberty. You could eat in different restaurants and have a different kind of food every night in New York City. Our restaurants have foods from many different countries. You should also try the pizza in New York, because it's always delicious.

B. Read the *Before I Write* checklist. Make notes on the lines below.

Before I Write

▶ Study the model.

▶ Think about things to do in my city.

▶ Make notes about my city.

1. What a visitor should do first in my city:

   _____

2. What else a visitor could do:

   _____

3. Where and what a visitor should eat in my city:

   _____

   _____

Writing

WRITE THIS!

Read the *While I Write* checklist. Look at your notes from page 145 and write your paragraph.

While I Write

▶ Use *should* with a verb to tell about important things to see or do.

*First, you **should** visit the Empire State Building.*

▶ Use *could* to make suggestions.

*Next, you **could** visit an art museum.*

▶ Use *because* to tell why or give a reason.

*You should also try the pizza in New York, **because** it's always delicious.*

AFTER YOU WRITE

A. Read the *After I Write* checklist. Make corrections to your paragraph above.

After I Write

▶ Did I use *should* with a verb to tell about important things to see or do?

▶ Did I use *could* to make suggestions?

▶ Did I use *because* to tell why or give a reason?

B. Make a final copy of your paragraph in your notebook.

Chapter 18

It was too easy.

LISTENING AND READING

Read "The Test" on Student Book pages 198–199. Then complete
each sentence. Circle the letter of the correct answer.

1. Mr. Gomez thought the students looked

   _____ before the test.

   a. gloomy   **b.** relaxed

2. Liliana thought the _____ section was hard.

   a. comprehension   **b.** vocabulary

3. Pablo said, "I did _____ than I expected."

   a. better   **b.** worse

4. Mei and Carlos said the test was too easy, but they were only _____ Maria.

   a. worrying   **b.** teasing

5. Maria should just _____ and wait to see her grade.

   a. pass   **b.** relax

VOCABULARY

A. Match the words in the left-hand column with the words in the right-hand column.
Write the letters on the line.

____ **1.** wonder   **a.** understanding

____ **2.** exactly   **b.** not fail

____ **3.** gloomy   **c.** correctly, truly

____ **4.** pass   **d.** sad or blue

____ **5.** comprehension   **e.** have questions about

B. In your notebook, write a short dialogue between a teacher and a student.
Use each of the five vocabulary words from Exercise A.

Example: Teacher: *Why do you look so gloomy?*

             Student: *The test was very hard.*

Grammar 1

Comparatives and Superlatives: Irregular Adjectives

A. Complete the sentences. Use *better than*, *the best*, *worse than*, or *the worst*.

1. His new calculator is _____*better than*_____ his old one.

2. Sabrina's calculator is _____.

3. Eduardo's grade is _____ Alicia's.

4. Morgan's grade is _____.

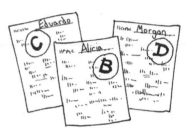

5. Cheesy Charlie's pizza is _____.

6. Pizza King's pizza is _____ Marvin's pizza.

B. Choose five activities and write them on the lines next to numbers 1–5. Then write about them using *better than*, *worse than*, *the best*, and *the worst*. Make true statements.

shopping	cleaning	singing	playing soccer
watching TV	exercising	doing gymnastics	dancing
reading comic books	baby-sitting	cooking	playing the guitar

Examples: *playing soccer*   *Playing soccer is better than dancing.*
                      watching TV   *Watching TV is the best activity.*

1. _____   _____

2. _____   _____

3. _____   _____

4. _____   _____

5. _____   _____

Grammar 2

Too and *not enough*

A. Write sentences using *too* and *not enough*. Use the words in parentheses.

1. I can't wear this jacket to the party.

   The sleeves _____*are too long*_____. (long)

   The sleeves _____*aren't short enough*_____. (short)

2. I don't want my friends to come over.

   My room _____. (dirty)

   My room _____. (clean)

3. I can't change the light bulb.

   I'm _____. (short)

   I'm _____. (tall)

4. I can't wear these jeans.

   These jeans _____. (small)

   These jeans _____. (big)

B. Write true statements using *too* or *not enough*.

Example: I (short / tall) . . .

I'm too short to be a good basketball player.

I'm not tall enough to to be a good basketball player.

1. The weather (hot/cool) . . .

   _____

   _____

2. The questions on the English test (easy/difficult) . . .

   _____

   _____

Word Study

Other Vowel Sound: /ûr/ as in *first*

A. Look at the pictures and sound out the words. Fill in the blanks with *ur, ir,* or *er*.

1. wint_____   **2.** sh_____t   **3.** moth_____   **4.** lett_____

5. b_____d   **6.** Th_____sday   **7.** g_____l   **8.** t_____tle

B. Read the poem. Circle the words with the vowel sound /ûr/.

My mother is a nurse.

She's wearing a long, gray skirt.

She carries a big, white purse.

She'll help you if you get hurt.

C. Choose two words from Exercise A. In your notebook, write a sentence using each word.

Example: *That's a pretty bird.*

Grammar 3

Statements with *used to*

Fill in the blanks with *used to* or *didn't use to*.

1. I _____*didn't use to*_____ like cheese, but now I do.

2. I _____ walk to school, but now I don't.

3. I _____ speak English, but now I do.

4. I _____ read comic books, but now I don't.

5. I _____ ride my bike a lot, but now I don't.

6. I _____ play the guitar, but now I do.

Yes/No Questions with *used to*

Write five *yes/no* questions about things you used to do. Use phrases
from the box or your own ideas. Then write true answers.

like broccoli	watch cartoons	read comic books	like Superman
walk to school	have a cat	play with dolls	speak English

1. A: *Did you use to watch cartoons a lot?*

   B: *Yes, I did. I used to watch Scooby Doo.*

2. A: _____

   B: _____

3. A: _____

   B: _____

4. A: _____

   B: _____

5. A: _____

   B: _____

6. A: _____

   B: _____

Reading

A. Read "The Last Day" on Student Book pages 204–205.
Then answer the questions. Write complete sentences.

1. What was the surprise in Mr. Gomez's classroom?

   _____

2. Which students passed the test?

   _____

3. What couldn't Maria believe?

   _____

4. How did Maria use to be?

   _____

5. How is Maria now?

   _____

B. Complete each sentence. Use a word from the box. Write one letter on
each line. Then write the circled letters to complete the sentence.

congratulations	grade	stunned	tease	world

1. There are many countries in the ◯◯__ __ __.

2. He was very, very surprised. He was __ __ __ __ ◯ __ __ ◯.

3. Tell me the truth. Don't __ ◯ __ __ __ me.

4. You passed the test! __ __ __ __ ◯ __ __ __ __ __ ◯ __ ◯ __!

5. What's your ◯ __ __ __ __? Did you pass the test?

Maria was __ __ __ __ __ __ __ __ __ how she did on the English test.

Writing

BEFORE YOU WRITE

A. Read the paragraph below.

> Sophie used to live in Haiti. She lived in a small town by the ocean. The beach was near her house, and she used to go swimming a lot. At home, she spoke Haitian Creole, but at school her classes were in French. Sophie loved Haiti, but life there was difficult for her family, so Sophie and her parents came to the United States last year. It was not easy at first. Sophie didn't speak English very well and she didn't have any friends here. She used to be sad a lot. Then Sophie started going to classes at Washington School. Now she has a lot of friends, her English is getting better, and she's really happy to be living in the United States.

B. Read the *Before I Write* checklist. Make notes on the lines below.

Before I Write

▶ Study the model.

▶ Imagine that Tomás is a new student in class. Think of a story about where he used to live and what brought him to my school.

▶ Make notes about Tomás.

1. Where Tomás used to live:

_____

2. What Tomás did and what language(s) he spoke:

_____

3. Why Tomás came to my school and how he feels now:

_____

Writing

WRITE THIS!

Read the *While I Write* checklist. Look at your notes from page 153 and write your story about Tomás.

While I Write

▶ Use *used to* to tell about things that were true in the past but aren't true now.
  *Sophie **used to** live in Haiti.*

▶ Use connecting words like *at first*, *later*, *then*, and *now* to show the order of events.
  ***Then** Sophie started going to classes at Washington School.*

▶ Include lots of details.
  She lived in a small town by the ocean.
  The beach was near her house.

AFTER YOU WRITE

A. Read the *After I Write* checklist. Make corrections to your paragraph above.

After I Write

▶ Did I use *used to* to tell about things that were true in the past but aren't true now?

▶ Did I use connecting words like *at first*, *later*, *then*, and *now* to show the order of events?

▶ Did I include lots of details?

B. Make a final copy of your paragraph in your notebook.

Reader's Companion

READER'S COMPANION

Life Science Use with Student Book pages 210–211

Summary: How Nature Works

Every forest, mountain, ocean, or other place in nature has a group of living and non-living things that work together. A group of living and non-living things that work together is called an ecosystem. The living things in the ecosystem are all part of a food chain. For example, a rabbit eats a plant, and then a fox eats the rabbit. The non-living things in the ecosystem are other things in nature that the living things need—for example, soil, water, air, and sunlight.

Visual Summary

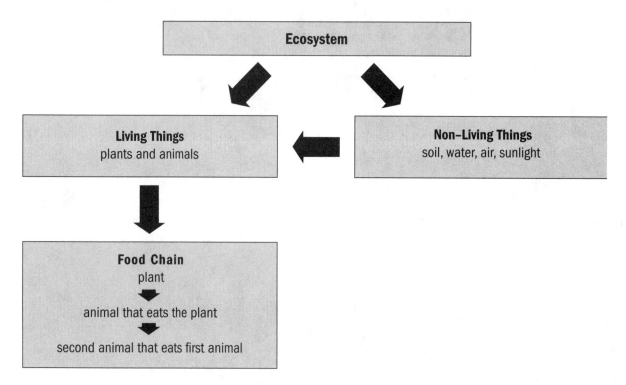

How Nature Works:
Ecosystems and Food Chains

Ecosystems are all around us. They are how **nature** works. Every place on Earth—every **forest**, mountain, and ocean—has an ecosystem. All living things, including **humans**, are part of an ecosystem.

Ecosystems

Ecosystems have both living and non-living things. Plants and animals are living things. Sunlight, air, rocks, and soil are non-living things.

The living things in an ecosystem need both non-living things and other living things. For example, plants need soil, water, and sunlight. Animals need air, water, and food. Animals' food can be plants, other animals, or both.

---

nature, the world and everything in it that people have not made, such as animals, weather, plants
forest, a place where lots of trees grow
humans, people

Use What You Know

Air is one thing that people need to stay alive. What are some others? Write down at least two things.

_____

_____

_____

Language Link

The prefix *non-* means "not." Circle a word that uses this prefix. What does the word mean?

MARK THE TEXT

_____

Learning Strategy: Compare

To compare is to see how two things are the same and how they are different. Underline what plants need and what animals need. Then compare what plants need to what animals need. Circle and write the thing that they both need.

MARK THE TEXT

_____

The first paragraph gives an example of a food chain. **MARK THE TEXT** Underline and number the three things that make up that food chain. Then explain what a food chain is.

_____

_____

_____

Words that compare sometimes end in -er. Circle the word **MARK THE TEXT** that ends in -er in the second paragraph on this page. Then tell what it compares.

_____

_____

Food Chains

Plants, the animals that eat them, and the animals that eat those animals are all part of a food chain. In a food chain, each living thing is linked to the other living things in the chain. For example, a food chain can begin with a plant. The plant grows leaves. Then, a rabbit eats some of the leaves. Next, a fox eats the rabbit.

Rabbits need plants to live. Foxes need smaller animals to live. Every part of the food chain is important in an ecosystem.

> Draw a food chain that starts with a plant and ends with a person. Show at least one animal in between.

READER'S COMPANION

Physical Science Use with textbook pages 212–213.

Summary: The Universe

The universe is a huge wide-open space that is made up of billions of galaxies. Each galaxy contains billions of stars. The universe contains planets. Earth is one of the small planets. It goes around a medium-size star called the sun. Other planets also go around the sun. The sun and the planets that go around it form a solar system. Our solar system is part of the Milky Way galaxy, which has about 200 billion other stars besides the sun. And the Milky Way is just one of the billions of galaxies in the universe.

Visual Summary

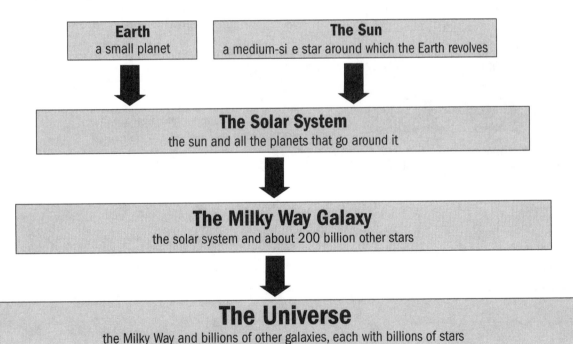

The Universe:
Earth and the Milky Way

How large is the universe? The universe has billions of galaxies, and each galaxy has billions of stars. Our Earth is one small **planet** in this galaxy of stars.

The Stars

From Earth, stars look like small lights in the night sky. But each star is really a giant ball of hot gas. Many stars are in small groups. The Big Dipper is a famous example of a group of stars.

Our sun is a medium-size star. Its core, or center, is very hot. The heat in the core of the sun reaches up to 15 million degrees centigrade (27 million degrees Fahrenheit)!

---

planet, a very large round object in space that moves around a star

The Solar System

Our sun is at the center of a solar system. In a solar system, planets go around a sun.

Nine planets go around our sun: Mercury, Venus, Earth, Mars, Jupiter, Saturn, Uranus, Neptune, and Pluto.

The Galaxy

Our solar system is part of the Milky Way galaxy. A galaxy is a very large group of stars. How large? There are about 200 billion (200,000,000,000) stars in the Milky Way galaxy! And the Milky Way is just one of billions of other galaxies in the universe.

> Draw a picture of our solar system. Show the planets going around the sun. Label each planet.

Language Link

MARK THE TEXT

Many English words come from a language called Latin. In Latin, the word for sun is "sol." Circle the word in the first paragraph that contains the Latin word sol. Then explain what the solar system has to do with the sun.

_____

_____

_____

Check Your Understanding

MARK THE TEXT

Underline the words that tell what a galaxy is. Which galaxy is Earth a part of?

_____

_____

READER'S COMPANION

Math Use with textbook pages 214–215.

Summary: Solving Word Problems

A word problem is a math problem that is expressed in words. To solve a word problem, you need to rewrite it as a regular math problem. First, turn it into numbers. Then decide on the math operation to use—addition, subtraction, multiplication, or division. Finally, solve the problem. Be sure to check your answer.

Visual Summary

How to Solve a Word Problem

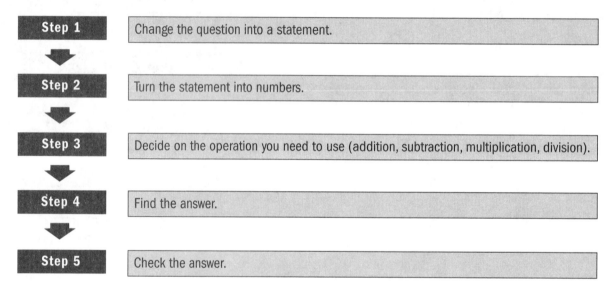

Step 1	Change the question into a statement.
Step 2	Turn the statement into numbers.
Step 3	Decide on the operation you need to use (addition, subtraction, multiplication, division).
Step 4	Find the answer.
Step 5	Check the answer.

Solving Word Problems: Mathematics in Everyday Life

Word problems are mathematical problems that are expressed in words. Many word problems are about situations that happen in everyday life. Here is an example of a word problem:

> Movie tickets cost $6 each. Mark has $40. How many tickets can Mark buy?

Rewriting Word Problems

You can **solve** word problems by rewriting them. Use these five steps:

1. **Rewrite the question.**

   Change the question into a statement. Leave a blank space for the answer:

   > Mark can buy _____ $6 movie tickets with $40.

2. **Find the numbers you need.**

   The numbers in this problem are 40 and 6. Write them on a piece of paper.

---

solve, to find the answer to something

Use What You Know

Think of the times when you use math in everyday life. Describe one thing you do where you use math.

_____

_____

_____

Check Your Understanding

Circle the example of a word problem. Then explain what a word problem is.

_____

_____

_____

Learning Strategy: Selective Attention

Use selective attention to focus on key ideas and words. Find and underline the key numbers in the statement.

Check Your Understanding

Circle the four math operations. Which do you use to show how many times one number goes into another?

_____

Language Link

The word *equation* is related to the word *equal*. Circle the symbol for "equal" or "equals" in the equation. Then, using the word *equals*, explain what an equation is.

MARK THE TEXT

_____

_____

_____

Check Your Understanding

Read Steps 4 and 5. Then explain what the *r* in the equation stands for and what it means.

_____

_____

_____

3. **Choose the operation.**

> **Mathematical Operations**
>
> + Addition   − Subtraction
>
> x Multiplication   ÷ Division

To find the answer, you need to know how many times 6 goes into 40. You need to use division. What is 40 divided by 6?

4. **Find the answer.**

Write the **equation:**

> $40 \div 6 = 6\,r\,4$

Answer: Mark can buy *6 movie tickets* with $40. There is a remainder of 4, so *$4 is left*.

5. **Check your answer.**

Check a division answer by multiplying. Then add the **remainder:**

> $6 \times 6 = 36$
> $36 + 4 = 40$

---

equation, a mathematical statement using numbers and an equal sign

remainder, the amount that is left when a number cannot be divided evenly

Simplifying Word Problems

Another **strategy** for solving word problems is **simplifying**. One way to simplify is to cross out unnecessary information. Look at the information crossed out in this problem:

> ~~The Posadas want to buy a house. They want to know the size of the land that the house is built on. The yard around the house is~~ 36 meters long by 28.5 meters wide. How many square meters ~~is the land~~?

After you cross out the unnecessary information, what remains? The numbers and the words "long," "wide," and "square meters." This tells us that the problem is about *area*. You know that area is length times (x) width. Now you can write and solve the equation.

$$36 \times 28.5 = 1{,}026 \text{ (square meters)}$$

---

strategy, a plan for doing something
simplifying, making easier to understand

Look at **Use What You Know** on page 163. How did you need math to solve this problem? Write the word problem. Then use the five steps to show how the problem was solved.

Learning Strategy: Selective Attention

Use selective attention to focus on the key ideas and words in this math problem. What are two key words and two key numbers in this math problem?

_____

_____

Language Link

The prefix *un-* means "not." Circle a word in the first paragraph that has this prefix. What does the word mean?

MARK THE TEXT

_____

_____

Check Your Understanding

Which mathematical operation do you use to find area?

_____

READER'S COMPANION

Literature Use with textbook pages 216–217.

Summary: Poetry

   Poetry often uses images. These are words that help you picture things in your mind. Similes and metaphors can help create images. A simile compares two unlike things using *like* or *as*. A metaphor also compares two unlike things, but it does not use *like* or *as*. It says one thing *is* another thing. The poem "A Fleeting Dozen" by Jorge Luján creates images that show us things in a fresh, new way.

Visual Summary

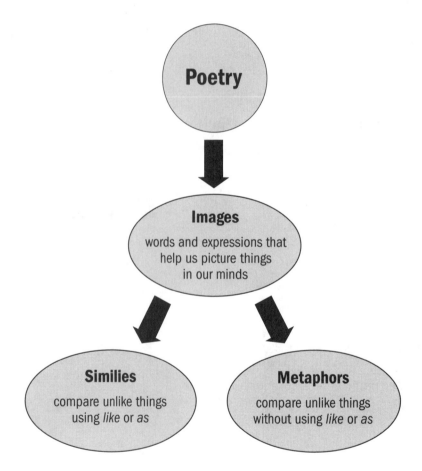

Poetry:
Understanding Images

Poetry uses words that make you feel things and let you see pictures in your mind. In a poem, the words may let you "see" a cat, or "hear" a flute, or even "smell" a lemon.

Figures of Speech: Similes and Metaphors

Many poems use **figures of speech** to create images, or pictures. A simile uses *like* or *as* to compare two unlike things: "Like a cat she moved quickly through the crowded hallway." A metaphor links two things without using *like* or *as*: "The stars were bright diamonds in the dark sky above."

In poetry, similes and metaphors **reveal** something new. They give us a fresh way of looking at something we already know.

---

figures of speech, groups of words that work together to compare one thing with another
reveal, show something not seen before

Read this poem.

A Fleeting Dozen

1   I put twelve oranges on the table:

      one rolled away like a **setting** sun,

3   another came to rest on a chair,

      two or three remain there in the middle

5   and the seven that were left

      are still speeding

7   through the open pathways of my mind.

—Jorge Luján
(translated from Spanish by John Oliver
and Simon and Rebecca Parfitt)

Understanding the Poem

To understand a poem, you should read it several times. Each time, stop and think about the words. What images do they create in your mind? How do the images make you feel?

---

fleeting, passing quickly; lasting for a very short time
dozen, a group of twelve
setting, sinking down

Learning Strategy: Images, Similes, and Metaphors

Underline the simile in the second line of the poem. Circle the two unlike things that it compares. Even though they are not alike in most ways, in what way are the two things alike?

MARK THE TEXT

_____

_____

_____

Check Your Understanding

The poem tells what happened to twelve oranges. Number the oranges in lines 2–5 to show that there are still twelve.

MARK THE TEXT

Learning Strategy: Images, Similes, and Metaphors

The last paragraph on this page ends in two questions. To answer the first question, put boxes around at least two images in the poem. Then answer the other question on the lines below. Explain how the images make you feel.

MARK THE TEXT

_____

_____

_____

_____

Read the first two lines of the poem again. Think about the simile, "One rolled away like a setting sun." Why do you think the poet is comparing one of the oranges to the setting sun? Reread the rest of the poem. What happened to the seven oranges—the "seven that were left"? What image do you "see" at the end?

Your answers might be different from your classmates' answers. Not everyone interprets, or explains, the meaning of a poem the same way, and that is okay. Some poems are hard to interpret, but we can still enjoy the images they create.

> Draw the painting that the poem describes. Show the images that you pictured in your mind.

Language Link

In most English words, a single *e* at the end of a word is silent. But the single *e* at the end of *simile* has a long *e* sound. It rhymes with *me*. Circle the word *simile* in the first paragraph, and put a line over the *e* to show that it has a long *e* sound. Say the word out loud. Then circle six more words on this page that have a long *e* sound. Put a line over the letter or letters that have the long *e* sound. Say all six words out loud.

MARK THE TEXT

Check Your Understanding

Underline the word or words that tell you what *interpret* means. If you have trouble interpreting a poem, what should you do?

MARK THE TEXT

_____

_____

_____

_____

READER'S COMPANION

Social Studies Use with textbook pages 218–219.

Summary: The United States

You can learn a lot about the United States from a map. A map has a compass that helps you figure out directions—north, east, south, and west. It also has a scale that helps you figure out the distances between places. Maps usually show the location of political features like countries, states, and cities. Maps can also show the location of physical features like mountains and oceans.

Visual Summary

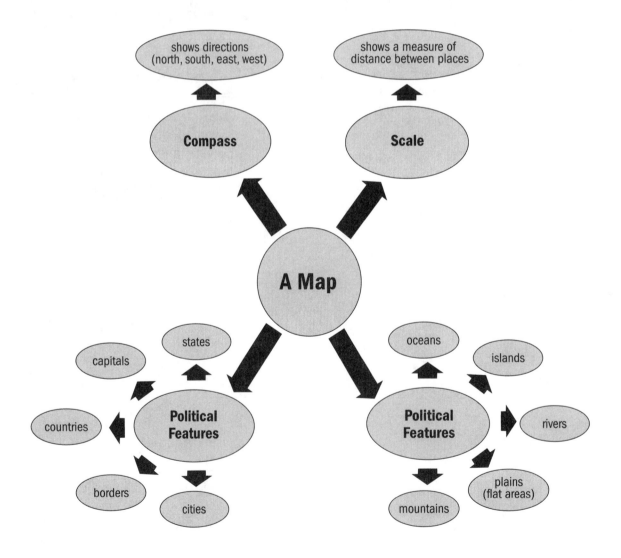

The United States: Reading Maps of Our Country

The United States of America is a very large country. It stretches from the Pacific Ocean to the Atlantic Ocean. We can learn more about this country by studying its maps.

How to Read a Map

A map's compass shows direction, and its scale shows distance. The *N* on the compass shows *north*. From north, you can find south (down), east (right), and west (left).

Look at the map on the next page and find the scale. The scale helps you measure the distance between places. For example, you can see that New York City is about 1,300 kilometers (800 miles) from Chicago. About how far is it from New York City to Los Angeles?

Use What You Know

Write down the names of three big cities in the United States. Do you know what states they are in? If so, write those too.

_____

_____

_____

Learning Strategy: Preview

When you preview, you look at pages before you read them. Look for headings, art, and terms in dark print. This will give you a better idea of the important information on the page. Preview the rest of this page, and circle the headings it contains. What information do the headings show will be on the page?

_____

_____

Check Your Understanding

Look at the map on the next page. Put the edge of a piece of paper up against the scale, and mark off the start and end on the piece of paper. Then put the same edge between Chicago and Santa Fe. About how far is it from Chicago to Santa Fe?

_____

_____

Language Link

The suffix -al means "of" or "related to." Circle two words in the first paragraph that use this suffix. Then explain what the words mean.

MARK THE TEXT

_____

_____

_____

Check Your Understanding

Use the compass on the map to figure out where south is. Which city on the map is furthest south?

_____

Political Map

Political features on a map show the **borders** of countries and states. There are forty-eight states in the **continental** United States. Alaska and Hawaii are not in the continental United States. Look at the map again and find these two states.

A political map also shows cities and capitals. The government of a country or state is in its capital city. Find Washington, D.C., the capital of the United States, on the map.

_____

borders, places where one country or state ends and another begins
continental, on the main part of the continent of North America

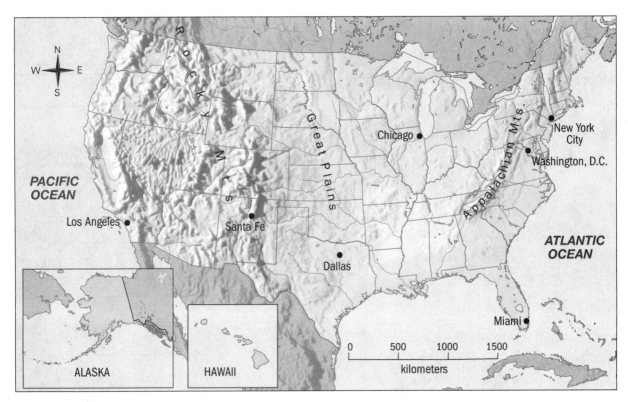

▲ Political and physical map of the United States

Physical Map

Physical features on a map show the landforms of a country. There is a long mountain range in the east called the Appalachian Mountains. There is another one in the west called the Rocky Mountains. Find these mountain **ranges** on the map on page 172.

The Great Plains region is in the center of the United States. Plains are flat areas with few or no hills. Many of the largest farms in the United States are here. Find the Great Plains on the map.

_____

ranges, groups of related mountains

Draw your own map of a country other than the United States. Show the capital and at least two other cities. Also label at least two bodies of water or mountain ranges.

Preview this page before you read it. Circle the heading **MARK THE TEXT** on the page. What kind of information shown on maps is this page about?

_____

Check Your Understanding

Physical features also include oceans, rivers, and other bodies of water. Look at the map on page 172. What two bodies of water are labeled on the map?

_____

_____

Language Link

The word *plain* can mean "simple" or "a flat place." What does it mean in the last paragraph?

_____

_____

READER'S COMPANION

History Use with textbook pages 220–221.

Summary: Martin Luther King Jr.

Martin Luther King Jr. was a great American hero. He was born in Atlanta, Georgia, in 1929. At that time, African Americans did not have the same rights as Caucasian Americans. The Civil Rights movement fought to change that situation. King joined this movement and later became its leader. He made his famous *I Have a Dream* speech at a big demonstration in Washington, D.C., in 1963. King's work helped get new laws passed that gave equal rights to all Americans. When he was killed in 1968, people all over the world were upset.

Visual Summary

Martin Luther King Jr.

1929	was born in Atlanta, Georgia
1944	graduated high school and went on to college at age fifteen
1954	joined others in Civil Rights movement
1962	became leader of Civil Rights movement
1963	gave *I Ha e a Dream* speech in Washington, D.C.
1968	was killed in Memphis, Tennessee

Martin Luther King Jr.: An American Hero

Martin Luther King Jr. was an American **hero**. His dream was for all people to have equal **rights**. He fought for that dream and helped to make it happen.

King's Early Life

Martin Luther King Jr. was born on January 15, 1929, in Atlanta, Georgia. At that time, African Americans were **segregated** from **Caucasians** in some states. They had to go to separate schools, and they had to eat at separate restaurants. They also had to sit at the back of buses.

Martin Luther King Jr. was a very good student. At fifteen, he finished high school. He went on to study at several colleges and **universities**. When he received his Ph.D, he became "Doctor King."

_____
hero, a brave person
rights, what is and should be allowed by law
segregated, kept apart
Caucasians, white people
universities, colleges

Check Your Understanding

Underline what Dr. King and the other people were fighting for. Then write a sentence explaining what the Civil Rights movement was.

MARK THE TEXT

_____

_____

_____

Learning Strategy: Relate

How do you think you would have felt if you were at the big demonstration in 1963? Write a sentence telling your feelings.

_____

_____

_____

Language Link

The prefix *il-* means "not." Circle the word in the second paragraph that uses this prefix. Then write what the word means.

MARK THE TEXT

_____

_____

Dr. King, Civil Rights Leader

In 1954, Dr. King joined other people who were fighting for equal rights for all Americans. The fight they led became known as the Civil Rights movement.

By 1962, Dr. King was the leader of the Civil Rights movement. In 1963, there was a large **demonstration** in Washington, D.C. More than 250,000 people came to the demonstration. Dr. King gave his most famous speech there, called *I Have a Dream*. The next year, one of Dr. King's dreams came true. **Congress** passed a law called the Civil Rights Act. This law made it illegal to **discriminate** against people because of their color, religion, or the country they came from.

---

demonstration, a gathering to show people's feelings about an issue or a cause
Congress, the part of the U.S. government that passes laws
discriminate, to treat a person or group unfairly

On April 4, 1968, Dr. King was **assassinated** in Memphis, Tennessee. People all over the world were shocked and saddened by the death of this American hero. His courage and leadership helped millions of people and changed the United States forever.

_____

assassinated, murdered for political reasons

> Draw a cartoon showing your feelings about the Civil Rights movement. Before you start, you may want to look at some political cartoons in newspapers or on the Internet.

Check Your Understanding

Underline the two qualities that helped make Martin Luther King Jr. a hero. Why were so many people affected by his death?

_____

_____

_____

_____

Learning Strategy: Relate

Martin Luther King Jr. dreamed about making the world a better place. Tell three things that you would do to make the world better today.

_____

_____

_____

_____

_____

_____

Grammar
Reference
and Practice

Present Tense of *be* (Student Book page 21)

Use the **present tense** to give facts and tell about things that happen regularly.
The verb *be* has three present-tense forms: *am*, *is*, and *are*.

I	am		We		
You	are	from El Salvador.	You	are	from El Salvador.
He / She / It	is		They		

To make a negative statement with *be*, add *not* after the verb.
   Mr. Gomez **is not** from El Salvador.   Mr. Gomez **isn't** from El Salvador.

Contractions:	
I am = I'm	we are = we're
you are = you're	you are = you're
he is = he's	they are = they're
she is = she's	
it is = it's	

A. Complete the sentences with the correct form of *be*. Use contractions.

1. (We) _____*We're*_____ students at Wilson School.

2. (She) _____ in our class.

3. (It) _____ a blue backpack.

4. (You) _____ my sister.

5. (He) _____ from Mexico.

6. (They) _____ nervous.

7. (I) _____ your new teacher.

B. Change each statement from affirmative to negative. Use pronouns. Use contractions.

1. Kim is a student in our school. _*She's not a student in our school.*_____

2. Maria and Carmen are sisters. _____

3. Mr. Gomez is our math teacher. _____

4. Luz and I are from the United States. _____

5. The notebook is on the desk. _____

Grammar Reference and Practice   **179**

Present Tense of *have* (Student Book pages 30–31)

The verb *have* has two present-tense forms: *have* and *has*.

I You	**have**	a brother.	We You They	**have**	a brother.
He / She / It	**has**				

To make a negative statement with *have*, use *do not have* or *does not have*. Do not use *has* in a negative statement.

You **do not have** math now.
She **does not have** seven classes.

Use the contractions *don't* and *doesn't* in speaking and informal writing.

You **don't** have math now.　　　(do not = don't)
She **doesn't** have seven classes.　　(does not = doesn't)

A. Complete the sentences with the correct form of *have*.

1. You and I _____*have*_____ English class together. (have / has)

2. Mr. Gomez _____ twelve students in his class. (have / has)

3. The students _____ different math teachers. (have / has)

4. You _____ lunch after me. (have / has)

5. We _____ the same schedules on Tuesday and Thursday. (have / has)

6. Maria _____ almost the same schedule as Liliana. (have / has)

7. I _____ a new math teacher. (have / has)

B. Change each statement from affirmative to negative. Use *don't have* or *doesn't have*.

1. They have math class after lunch.　　*They don't have math class after lunch.*

2. Mr. Gomez has four new students.　　*Mr. Gomez doesn't have four new students.*

3. Maria has a new P.E. teacher.　　_____

4. The girls have the same schedule.　　_____

5. We have science together.　　_____

6. I have a sister.　　_____

Present Tense of Regular Verbs (Student Book page 63)

A regular verb has two forms in the present tense.

I	**like**		We	**like**	music.
You		music.	You		
He / She / It	**likes**		They		

To make a negative statement in the present tense, use *do not* or *does not* before the base form of the verb. Use the contractions *don't* and *doesn't* in speaking and informal writing.

I **do not speak** Spanish.   I **don't speak** Spanish.

He **does not need** a map.   He **doesn't need** a map.

A. Complete the sentences. Use the correct form of the verb from the box to make affirmative statements.

need   live   eat   like   borrow   listen

1. My friends and I _____*eat*_____ lunch in the cafeteria at the same time.

2. The boys _____ directions to the party.

3. I _____ next to the school.

4. My father _____ to music every night after dinner.

5. Carmen _____ all the things her brother likes.

6. My sister _____ my new backpack every Sunday.

B. Change the affirmative statements in Exercise A to negative statements.

1. *My friends and I don't eat lunch in the cafeteria at the same time.* _____

2. _____

3. _____

4. _____

5. _____

6. _____

Past Tense of *be* (Student Book page 75)

Use the **past tense** to tell about events that happened in the past and are completed.
The verb *be* has two past-tense forms: *was* and *were*.

Mei **was** in the gym.
You **were** at school yesterday.

To make a past-tense negative statement with *be*, add *not* after the verb. In speaking and informal writing, use the contractions *wasn't* and *weren't*.

Mei **was not** in the gym.	Mei **wasn't** in the gym.
You **were not** at school yesterday.	You **weren't** at school yesterday.

Look at the students' schedules. Complete the sentences with *was*, *were*, *wasn't*, or *weren't*.

Vic's Schedule	Melinda's Schedule	Jon's Schedule
9:30 P.E.	9:30 science	9:30 P.E.
10:15 English	10:15 P.E.	10:40 science
11:30 lunch	11:30 lunch	11:30 math
12:15 science	12:15 English	12:15 lunch
1:15 music	1:15 music	1:15 music
2:00 math	2:00 math	2:00 English

1. All the students _____*were*_____ in school yesterday.

2. Melinda _____ in P.E. at 9:30.

3. Vic and Melinda _____ in math together at 2:00.

4. Jon _____ at lunch with Vic and Melinda at 11:30.

5. All of the students _____ in different science classes yesterday.

6. Vic and Jon _____ in P.E. with Melinda at 10:15.

7. Jon _____ in math at 11:30.

8. All of the students _____ in music together at 1:15.

9. Vic and Melinda _____ in the same English class.

10. Vic _____ in P.E. and music with Jon.

11. Jon _____ in science, math, or English with Vic and Melinda.

Name _____ Date _____

Present Continuous Tense (Student Book pages 84–85)

Use the **present continuous tense** to tell about something that is happening right now.
To form the present continuous tense, use the present tense of *be* and the base form
of the verb + **-ing**. In speaking and informal writing, use contractions.

I **am reading** a book.   **I'm reading** a book.

To make an information question, place the subject between the two parts of the verb.

What **is** she **reading**?

Remember that some verbs have special spelling rules when adding **-ing**.
If a verb ends in a silent **e**, drop the **e** before adding **-ing**.

writ**e** ⟶ **writing**

If a one-syllable verb ends in a consonant-vowel-consonant (CVC) pattern, double the last
consonant before adding **-ing** (except when the final consonant is *w*, *x*, or *y*).

get ⟶ **getting**

A. Fill in the chart. Write the present continuous form of the verbs.

1. speak ⟶ *speaking*	**5.** sit ⟶ _____
2. use ⟶ _____	**6.** listen ⟶ _____
3. point ⟶ _____	**7.** sweep ⟶ _____
4. eat ⟶ _____	**8.** write ⟶ _____

B. Read each answer. Write the questions. Use *what's* or *what are*.

1. _What's Luz eating?_____ (Luz)

She's eating lunch.

2. _____ (Anna and Jon)

They're writing their names.

3. _____ (Kim)

She's hitting the ball.

4. _____ (Rosa)

She's making cookies.

Simple Present Tense and Present Continuous Tense (Student Book page 94)

Use the **simple present tense** to give facts and tell about things that happen regularly.
I **walk** to school every morning.

Use the **present continuous tense** to tell about an action that is happening right now.
I **am walking** to school with my friends.

A. Read each sentence. Check **simple present** if the action happens regularly.
Check **present continuous** if the action is happening right now.

	Simple Present	Present Continuous
1. I wash my hair every day.	✔	☐
2. The girls play soccer every Saturday.	☐	☐
3. Mr. Smith's family lives next to the new high school.	☐	☐
4. Kim is baby-sitting the children.	☐	☐
5. Carmen and Carlos are getting ready for their party.	☐	☐
6. Our favorite TV show is on every Thursday night.	☐	☐
7. We turn off all the lights at night.	☐	☐
8. They are cleaning the kitchen now.	☐	☐

B. Complete the sentences with the simple present or present continuous form of the verb.

1. Julio _____ his dog every morning. (walk)

2. The soccer team _____ at the new field now. (play)

3. I _____ my grandmother every Saturday. (call)

4. The Brown family _____ dinner at a new restaurant now. (eat)

5. Lucinda _____ the guitar in her room right now. (play)

6. Maria _____ every day after school. (study)

7. Now the students _____ their hands to answer the question. (raise)

8. Carmen and Carlos _____ their rooms now. (clean)

Past Tense of Regular Verbs (Student Book page 104)

To make the past tense of most regular verbs, add **-ed** to the base form.
  need ⟶ **needed**

Some regular verbs have special spelling rules in the past tense.
If a verb ends in a silent **e**, just add **-d**.
  danc**e** ⟶ **danced**

If a verb ends in a consonant + y, change the y to **i** before adding **-ed**.
  stud**y** ⟶ **studied**

A. Write the past-tense form of the verbs.

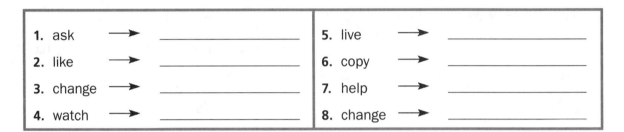

1. ask ⟶ _____   **5.** live ⟶ _____

2. like ⟶ _____   **6.** copy ⟶ _____

3. change ⟶ _____   **7.** help ⟶ _____

4. watch ⟶ _____   **8.** change ⟶ _____

B. Complete the sentences. Use the past-tense form of a word from the box.

borrow	study	want	dance	need	clean	introduce	play

1. My friends ____*wanted*____ new backpacks for the first day of school.

2. The boys and girls _____ to music at Carmen and Carlos's party.

3. I _____ last night for the English test.

4. Jon's grandmother _____ eggs and milk from the store to make the cookies.

5. The children _____ baseball at the park last Friday.

6. You _____ me to your sister at the party.

7. The children _____ the house with their mother last Saturday.

8. I _____ my friend's calculator yesterday.

Past Tense of Irregular Verbs (Student Book page 105)

Many verbs have irregular forms in the past tense. We do not add **-ed** to make the past tense of these verbs.

Bic **ate** three slices of pizza.

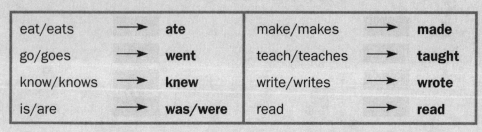

eat/eats	→	ate	make/makes	→	made
go/goes	→	went	teach/teaches	→	taught
know/knows	→	knew	write/writes	→	wrote
is/are	→	was/were	read	→	read

A. Complete the dialogues. Use the correct form of the verb. Use words from the chart.

1. **A:** Yesterday I _____*went*_____ shopping with my mother at the Garden State Mall. (go)

   B: I know. I _____ there, too. Remember? (be)

   A: Oh yeah! We _____ in the shoe store together. (be)

2. **A:** Mr. Jones _____ your grandfather. (know)

   B: Really?

   A: Yes. Your grandfather _____ Mr. Jones how to play the piano. (teach)

3. **A:** Mom _____ cookies for us last night. (make)

   B: I know. I _____ one this morning. (eat)

B. Look at Luis's schedule. Write sentences about what he did last week.

| Wednesday | Thursday | Friday | Saturday | Sunday |
| go to my brother's soccer game | write my science report | eat at Gino's with my friends | go to the movies with Becky | read my history book all day |

1. On Wednesday, _____*he went to his brother's soccer game.*_____ (go to)

2. On Thursday, _____. (write)

3. On Friday, _____. (eat)

4. On Saturday, _____. (go to)

5. On Sunday, _____. (read)

Past Tense: Negative Statements (Student Book page 107)

To make a negative statement in the past tense, add *did not* before the base form of the verb.
Do not use the *-ed* form or any irregular past-tense form.
    They **didn't talk** at the party.
    Bic **didn't eat** an enchilada.

A. Change each statement from affirmative to negative.

1. Cara's brother went to the movies with her yesterday.

   Carla's brother didn't go to the movies with her yesterday.

2. Min had a good time at the party.

   _____

3. Hannah's friends ate lunch with her in the school cafeteria.

   _____

4. You went out to dinner last night.

   _____

5. Marco studied at the library after school.

   _____

B. Look at the sentences you wrote about Luis on page 186, Exercise B. Change each
statement from affirmative to negative.

1. (go to)   *He didn't go to his brother's soccer game on Wednesday.*

2. (write)   _____

3. (eat)   _____

4. (go to)   _____

5. (read)   _____

C. Write two sentences about what you *didn't* do yesterday.

   Example: *I didn't go out to dinner.*

   1. _____

   2. _____

Past Continuous Tense (Student Book page 158)

Use the **past continuous tense** to tell about an action that was happening at a specific time in the past. To form the past continuous tense, use the past tense of *be* and the base form of the verb + *-ing*.

They **were eating** breakfast at 8:00.

To make a negative statement in the past continuous tense, add *not* between the form of *be* and the *-ing* verb. In speaking and informal writing, use the contractions *wasn't* and *weren't*.

I **was not studying**. ⟶ I **wasn't studying**.

A. Look at the chart. Write sentences about what the children were and weren't doing last weekend. Use the words in the box.

play	make	watch	ride	clean	paint	shop

	Saturday	**Sunday**
Jon		
Kim		
Jen		
Tania		

1. (Jon) *Jon was riding his bike last Saturday. He wasn't playing soccer.*

2. (Kim) _____

3. (Jen) _____

4. (Tania) _____

B. What were *you* doing last weekend? Write one affirmative statement and one negative statement.

1. _____

2. _____

Future Tense with *be going to* and *will* (Student Book pages 148 and 168)

Use the future tense with *be going to* to talk about the immediate future, to make predictions, and to tell about plans that were made before now. Use a present-tense form of *be* plus *going to* and the base form of a verb.

> She **is going to** watch TV tonight. She**'s going to** watch TV tonight.
> We **are going to** have a party next week. We**'re going to** have a party next week.

To make a negative statement about the future, use *not* and a present-tense form of *be*.

> She **is not going to** go to school tomorrow. She **isn't going to** go to school tomorrow.
> They **are not going to** have a party. They **aren't going to** have a party.

Another way to talk about the future is with *will* plus the base form of a verb. Use the future tense with *will* to give general facts about the future, to make promises, and to tell about sudden ideas or decisions.

> We **will** help you. We**'ll** help you.

To make a negative statement about the future, use *will not*. In speaking and informal writing, use the contraction *won't*.

> The club **will not** meet tomorrow. It **won't** meet tomorrow.

Look at the chart. Write sentences about what the children *are going to* or *will* do this weekend. Use *isn't*, *aren't*, or *won't* to write negative sentences.

	have a birthday	go to the library	baby-sit	buy clothes	visit a friend
Miranda	✔		✔	✔	✔
Delia			✔	✔	✔
Arturo	✔	✔			✔

1. Miranda and Arturo _____ *are going to have a birthday.* _____ (going to)

2. Arturo _____. (will, negative)

3. Miranda _____. (will)

4. Miranda _____. (going to, negative)

5. Delia _____. (going to)

6. Miranda and Delia _____. (will)

Grammar Reference and Practice **189**

Statements with *used to* (Student Book page 203)

> Use **used to** plus the base form of a verb to talk about something that was true or often happened in the past but is not true or does not happen in the present.
>   I **used to live** in a small town. Now I live in a big city.
>
> The negative form of **used to** is **didn't use to**.
>   I **didn't use to** like Japanese food, but now I do.

You are going to write about yourself. First, complete the phrases in the chart. Then write ten sentences about yourself.

used to	didn't use to
eat _enchiladas_	eat _salad_
play _____	play _____
borrow _____	borrow _____
listen _____	listen _____
want _____	want _____
watch _____	watch _____

Example: *I used to eat enchiladas for lunch every day.*

1. _____

2. _____

3. _____

4. _____

5. _____

Example: *I didn't use to eat salad for lunch, but now I do.*

1. _____

2. _____

3. _____

4. _____

5. _____

Handwriting
Practice

Write the capital letters.

A   A

B   B

C   C

D   D

E   E

F   F

G   G

H   H

I   I

J   J

K   K

L   L

M   M

Handwriting Practice

Name ____________________ Date __________

Write the capital letters.

N N

O O

P P

Q Q

R R

S S

T T

U U

V V

W W

X X

Y Y

Z Z

Write the small letters.

a

b

c

d

e

f

g

h

i

j

k

l

m

Handwriting Practice

Name ______________________ Date __________

Write the small letters.

n n

o o

p p

q q

r r

s s

t t

u u

v v

w w

x x

y y

z z

Write the numbers.

0   0   - - - -   - - - -   - - - -   - - - -   - - - -

1   1   - - - -   - - - -   - - - -   - - - -   - - - -

2   2   - - - -   - - - -   - - - -   - - - -   - - - -

3   3   - - - -   - - - -   - - - -   - - - -   - - - -

4   4   - - - -   - - - -   - - - -   - - - -   - - - -

5   5   - - - -   - - - -   - - - -   - - - -   - - - -

6   6   - - - -   - - - -   - - - -   - - - -   - - - -

7   7   - - - -   - - - -   - - - -   - - - -   - - - -

8   8   - - - -   - - - -   - - - -   - - - -   - - - -

9   9   - - - -   - - - -   - - - -   - - - -   - - - -

Handwriting Practice

Say the numbers.

1	2	3	4	5	6	7	8	9	10
11	12	13	14	15	16	17	18	19	20
21	22	23	24	25	26	27	28	29	30
31	32	33	34	35	36	37	38	39	40
41	42	43	44	45	46	47	48	49	50
51	52	53	54	55	56	57	58	59	60
61	62	63	64	65	66	67	68	69	70
71	72	73	74	75	76	77	78	79	80
81	82	83	84	85	86	87	88	89	90
91	92	93	94	95	96	97	98	99	100

Write the numbers.

1				5					
		13							20
						27			
	32								
								49	
		54							
61									
					76				
							88		
									100

Write the capital letters.

$\mathcal{A}$ $\mathcal{a}$ $\mathcal{a}$

$\mathcal{B}$ $\mathcal{B}$ $\mathcal{B}$

C C C

D $\mathcal{D}$ $\mathcal{D}$

E $\mathcal{E}$ $\mathcal{E}$

F $\mathcal{F}$ $\mathcal{F}$

G $\mathcal{G}$ $\mathcal{G}$

H $\mathcal{H}$ $\mathcal{H}$

I $\mathcal{l}$ $\mathcal{l}$

J $\mathcal{J}$ $\mathcal{J}$

K $\mathcal{K}$ $\mathcal{K}$

L $\mathcal{L}$ $\mathcal{L}$

M $\mathcal{m}$ $\mathcal{m}$

   Handwriting Practice

Name ______________________ Date ____________

Write the capital letters.

N *N* *N*

O *O* *O*

P *P* *P*

Q *Q* *Q*

R *R* *R*

S *S* *S*

T *T* *T*

U *U* *U*

V *V* *V*

W *W* *W*

X *X* *X*

Y *Y* *Y*

Z *Z* *Z*

Write the small letters.

_a_ _a_ _a_

_b_ _b_ _b_

_c_ _c_ _c_

_d_ _d_ _d_

_e_ _e_ _e_

_f_ _f_ _f_

_g_ _g_ _g_

_h_ _h_ _h_

_i_ _i_ _i_

_j_ _j_ _j_

_k_ _k_ _k_

_l_ _l_ _l_

_m_ _m_ _m_

Handwriting Practice

Name ______________________________ Date ____________

Write the small letters.

n n n

o o o

p p p

q q q

r r r

s s s

t t t

u u u

v v v

w w w

x x x

y y y

z z z

Name ____________________ Date __________

Write the capital and small letters.

Aaa Aaa Aaa

Bbb Bbb Bbb

Ccc Ccc Ccc

Ddd Ddd

Eee Eee

Fff Fff

Ggg Ggg

Hhh Hhh

Iii Iii

Jjj Jjj

Kkk Kkk

Lll Lll

Mmm Mmm

Write the capital and small letters.

Nnn   Nnn

Ooo   Ooo

Ppp   Ppp

Qqq   Qqq

Rrr   Rrr

Sss   Sss

Ttt   Ttt

Uuu   Uuu

Vvv   Vvv

Www   Www

Xxx   Xxx

Yyy   Yyy

Zzz   Zzz

Credits

Illustration Credits

Mike DiGiorgio 172; **John Hovell** 87 bottom; **Jane McCreary** 1–5, 7–9, 23, 28, 29, 33, 36–38 bottom, 39, 43 bottom, 45, 52, 60, 61, 76, 84, 92, 93, 100, 102 bottom, 103, 109, 111, 116, 117, 119, 121, 139 bottom, 148, 186, 189; **Christopher Pavely** 11, 16, 24, 27, 32, 35, 40, 43 top, 48, 51, 56, 59, 64, 72, 75, 80, 83, 87 top, 88, 91, 96, 99, 104, 107, 112, 115, 120, 123, 128, 131, 139 top, 143, 144, 147, 152; **William Waitzman** 12, 22, 30, 38 top, 46, 54, 62, 70, 78, 86, 94, 102 top, 110, 118, 126, 134, 142, 150, 182.

Photo Credits

13, 15, 17, 25, 31, 65 David Young-Wolff/PhotoEdit; 20, 44 Michael Newman/PhotoEdit; 21 Will Hart/PhotoEdit; 41 Gareth Brown/CORBIS; 47 Stockbyte; 49 IT Stock International/Stock Photo/Picture Quest; 53, 141 left Paul Barton/CORBIS; 55 Frank Siteman/Stock, Boston/Picture Quest; 57, 68, 85, 133, 141 right, 145 Getty Images; 63 Tony Freeman/PhotoEdit; 69 Randy Wells/CORBIS; 70 Richard Hamilton Smith/CORBIS; 73 Gareth Brown/CORBIS; 77 Michael Newman/PhotoEdit; 81 Will Hart/PhotoEdit; 89 CORBIS; 95 Richard Hutchings/PhotoEdit; 97 Food Pix/Getty Images; 101 AP/Wide World Photos; 105, 135 Bob Daemmrich/The Image Works; 108 Peter Beck/CORBIS; 113 Tony Freeman/PhotoEdit; 124 Jose Luis Pelaez, Inc./CORBIS; 125 Dave G. Houser/CORBIS; 127 Tom Stewart/CORBIS; 129 Dallas and John Heaton/CORBIS; 137, 151 Michael A. Keller/CORBIS; 140 Superstock; 149 Patrick Giardino/CORBIS; 153 Rick Friedman/CORBIS.